# SAUNTERING THE SPIRITUAL VARIANT OF THE CAMINO DE SANTIAGO

KENNETH CLINE

MOT-MOT PUBLISHING

Copyright © 2021 by Kenneth Cline

All rights reserved. No part of this book may be reproduced in any manner without written permission, except in the case of brief quotations embodied in critical articles and reviews.

The events related in this account are true, based on a walk undertaken by the author and his wife along the Spiritual Variant of the Caminho Português in May/June 2019.

ISBN: 978-0-9979415-9-3

Photos: Bina Cline, unless noted otherwise

Cover Photo: Combarro waterfront, by Bina Cline

❦ Created with Vellum

# DEDICATION

Again, for Bina, whose loving spirit and enthusiasm made it all possible.

*"I don't like either the word [hike] or the thing. People ought to saunter in the mountains - not 'hike!' Do you know the origin of that word saunter? It's a beautiful word. Away back in the middle ages, people used to go on pilgrimages to the Holy Land, and when people in the villages through which they passed asked where they were going they would reply, 'A la sainte terre', 'To the Holy Land.' And so they became known as sainte-terre-ers or saunterers. Now these mountains are our Holy Land, and we ought to saunter through them reverently, not 'hike' through them."*
— Naturalist John Muir

*Wherever you go, go with all your heart! – Confucius*

# PROLOGUE

*V*espers at 7 p.m., they said, but where, exactly?

Bina and I had been told, when we first checked into our room at the Mosteiro de Santa María da Armenteira, that Vespers would be held in a chapel just off the cloister. About 15 minutes before seven, we walked around the rectangular, colonnaded circuit. Several doors led into the two-story stone building enclosing the cloister's walkway, but none featured a sign saying something along the lines of, "Vespers here."

Had we misunderstood the directions? Surely an event to which the public was invited would be publicized with at least a sign. A woman in khaki pants and short sleeves walked up to us looking similarly puzzled. "Do you know if Vespers is in this place?" she asked, in slightly accented English, which I took to be Scandinavian.

I shrugged. "We think so, but nobody's here. Maybe it might be in the church?" A Baroque Era church fronted the left side of the monastery's main entrance.

The woman considered that suggestion and nodded briefly. "I go ask in geeft shop," she said, and turned to leave.

Getting impatient, I resolved to go around the quadrangle

turning doorknobs. Walking up to the nearest one, I pushed the handle down and nudged it open. The heavy wood creaked on its hinges to reveal a darkened room. Several people, arranged in pews, looked at me quizzically. In a lighted area off to the left, I could discern nuns seating themselves around an altar. By what interior passage had all these people arrived here while we were standing outside?

*There's a Vespers service here somewhere ...*

I beckoned to Bina, who called back the other woman. The three of us entered the room and took our places in the pews, just a few minutes before seven. With our presence, the congregation now totaled over 10, comprised of several nationalities, as we could detect from the whispered conversations. Eight nuns and one priest, most of them elderly, had taken seats in a semicircle of chairs around the altar. One of the nuns sat at a small electronic organ. Precisely on the hour, she began playing the opening notes of the liturgy as the others intoned the verses in Spanish.

Other than the references to *Dios* (God) and *El Señor* (the Lord),

Bina and I couldn't follow the Spanish in detail so we settled into our seats to relax into the solemn rhythm and majesty of the Vespers service. Earlier in the day, while walking around the church, cloister and surrounding garden, Bina had described the Armenteira Monastery to me as a "thin place." This is an old Christian Celtic term connoting a physical spot where the veil between this world and the eternal is at its thinnest, enabling you to sense the presence of God. Listening to the hypnotic syncopation of the liturgy, I began to get that "thin place" feeling myself.

The culmination of the service, for us, came when one of the nuns called for the *"peregrinos"* in the audience to step up front to receive a special blessing. She meant those attendees walking the pilgrimage route to Santiago de Compostela known as the *Camino de Santiago*, or Way of St. James — all of us, in fact. As we arranged ourselves around the altar, she went down the line asking our nationalities, which turned out to be French, Danish, German and Spanish, with Bina and me representing the U.S. She then read the following words, first in Spanish and then English, which is the language most of the non-Spaniards could follow:

"May the light and love of God bless and direct your steps.
May the roads rise up to meet you.
May you open your heart to silence.
And keep with gratitude the joyous remembrance of the good things that you have encountered.
May God carry you in his hands to the arms of St. James in Santiago.
And may you go back to your home full of light and joy."

The priest approached each of us to make the sign of the cross on our foreheads. Following our 2018 Camino, Bina and I had received a similar pilgrims blessing in the cathedral in Santiago de Compostela. This one struck us as more personal and moving, perhaps because we were in a smaller group. Standing at the altar with the other pilgrims gave us a sense of participating in something larger than ourselves, embraced by a tradition that went back a thousand years. For that brief moment, we each escaped from a narrow focus on *me* to a more universal human experience of *us*.

That pilgrim's blessing at the Armenteira Monastery proved to be one of the highlights of our 2019 Camino. During two weeks in June, we walked 160 km (100 miles) from Viana do Castelo on the northern Portuguese coast to Santiago de Compostela in Spanish Galicia. The latter part of that walk included a 43-km segment of trail known as the *Variante Espiritual,* or Spiritual Variant, which passes through Armenteira.

The following pages will describe the various stages of the Spiritual Variant and why this walk deserves consideration for pilgrims walking the Portuguese Way of the Camino de Santiago. As our vespers experience in Armenteira suggests, it's indeed possible for this trail to live up to its name.

# THE SECOND ACT

There's something about the Camino de Santiago that pulls at the heartstrings. In September 2018, my wife Bina and I completed our first passage on this pilgrimage, walking nearly 200 miles from Porto, Portugal, to Santiago de Compostela.[1] It wasn't long after we celebrated our arrival in front of the Santiago cathedral that we began thinking of a second act, which occurred the following May.

Two motivations spurred our return. First, we wanted to "give back" to the Camino by enlisting for a two-week stint as *voluntarios* (volunteers) in the Pilgrim's Office in Santiago.[2] We had enjoyed our Camino so much in 2018 that we sought to enable other pilgrims to enjoy the same experience. The typical way that people give back to the Camino is by serving as *voluntarios*, either in the *albergues* (hostels) scattered along the routes, or in the Pilgrim's Office.

Our second motivation was simply to do another Camino walk. This is not at all uncommon. Spend any time in Camino-related social media and you'll notice all the die-hard veterans who come back year after year. At least seven major Camino trails wend their way to Santiago de Compostela — beginning in

France, Portugal or Spain itself — with variations within those routes. Walking the Camino is something you can do repeatedly and still enjoy new territory.

For our second act in 2019, Bina and I decided to repeat some of the route from Portugal we had done the previous year but with one important addition: the Spiritual Variant. This is an alternate trail of the main Portuguese Camino route that branches off to the west, just north of the Spanish city of Pontevedra, and loops around a region known as O Salnés before rejoining the main route at the town of Pontecesures, near Padrón.

Several factors went into our thinking. Since we would begin our 2019 adventure with the two-week volunteer stint in Santiago, we wanted to follow that up with a relatively uncomplicated Camino walk. The 2018 journey had required an enormous amount of planning and research on our part. It was our first Camino, after all, and in no way did we want to replicate all that work. It was more convenient to repeat those parts of the Portuguese Coastal that we had enjoyed the most in 2018, with a few modifications. We knew the trail and most of the accommodations available along the way, so additional planning would be minimal.

We also knew, from our 2018 experience, that the Portuguese Camino very much aligned with our level of physical conditioning. The Portuguese is the easiest of all the major Camino routes because of its low elevations, particularly if you stick to the coast. From Porto north to the Spanish port of Vigo, you're mostly dealing with flat ground. This constituted an important consideration for Bina and me considering our ages (mid-60s for me, low 60s for her) and health (my lower back issues, her diabetes, asthma and high blood pressure).

We began our 2019 walk in Viana do Castelo, rather than Porto. During our 2018 Camino, we had pinpointed Viana as a town that we would like to revisit. After finishing our volunteer work in Santiago on June 3, we took a Spanish train to Vigo and then transferred to a Portuguese train that took us south to Viana. We stayed there in an Airbnb, enjoying lovely harbor views, until the 14th, when we began walking north up the Portuguese coast.

*Framing the view on northern Portugal coast.*

The first stage of this trek took us to Valença, on the Minho River, which marks Portugal's northern border with Spain. We had intended, at this point, to cross the river to the Spanish city of Tui and walk the remaining stretch of the central Portuguese route to Redondela, where the central merges with the coastal wending up from Vigo. We were aware, however, that the trail from Tui to Redondela gets bad marks for scenery, particularly the industrial stretch around O Porriño.

At the last minute, we opted to take the train to Vigo and resume our Camino from there to enjoy the forested walk to Redondela, which includes sweeping views of the Vigo River that we remembered so fondly from 2018. After staying the night in Redondela, two more days of walking brought us on June 22 to Pontevedra, the gateway to the Spiritual Variant.

Bina and I had considered adding the Spiritual Variant to our itinerary in 2018, based on its reputation as one of the most scenic portions of the entire Camino Portuguese. But since the Variant had been added to the "official" Camino routes only five years before, practical information about walking the trail was scarce.[3] Being Camino "newbies" in 2018, we found it easier to stick with the path most traveled, which continued north to Pontecesures via Caldas de Reis. Still, the question nagged at us: had we missed out on something?

The name itself can tantalize you, implying that this route is more "spiritual" than the others. How can that be? Most Camino routes abound in medieval churches, chapels and shrines, as well as breath-taking natural views of mountains, coastline or Spain's famous *meseta* (interior plateau). If you're looking for spiritual places — however you want to define that — you'll find plenty on most parts of the Camino de Santiago.

The only way to know for sure was simply to place one foot in front of the other and have a look for ourselves. In 2019, Bina and I were determined to find out what, if anything, was distinctive about the Spiritual Variant.

---

1. This story is related in our previous book, *Sauntering to Santiago: The Camino de Santiago for Slow Walkers.*
2. See Appendix One, "Volunteering in the Pilgrim's Office."
3. The best source for the Spiritual Variant at the time was the book by Roy Uprichard, *Stone and Water: Walking the Spiritual Variant of the Camino Portugues,* Amazon 2018.

# NAMING NAMES ON THE CAMINO

*B*efore resuming the story of our journey, it might be helpful to provide some perspective on the Camino de Santiago itself, and how the modern selection of officially sanctioned routes developed.

The Camino originated nearly 1,200 years ago to serve a specific purpose: pilgrimage to the reputed burial place of St. James the Apostle.[1] This site, located on a remote hillside in northwestern Spain, became a shrine in the Middle Ages. The city subsequently built around it took the name Santiago de Compostela and began attracting pilgrims from all over Europe.

By the 12th century, Santiago had become one of Christendom's top three pilgrimage sites, after Jerusalem and Rome. Men and women of every social standing, including a queen of Portugal, walked by various trails to the cathedral at Santiago to seek penance for their sins by visiting the Apostle's tomb. After fulfilling this obligation, they would turn around and walk back home.

Some of these medieval routes saw more pilgrim traffic than others. The 12th-century Codex Calixtinus, which is considered the earliest of Camino "guidebooks," lists four roads that originated in France and converged on Puente la Reina, in northern Spain. From there, a well-traveled trail continued to Santiago de Compostela via Burgos, Carrión de Los Condes, Sahagún, León and Astorga. This formed the basis for the Camino Francés, the most popular of modern Camino paths.

As a general rule, however, medieval pilgrim routes were, literally, all over the map — far from the carefully delineated segments detailed in modern guidebooks. The aspiring pilgrim would simply leave his or her house — wherever that was located in Europe — and start walking in the general direction of Santiago de Compostela. Road selection would take in terrain and safety considerations. Which paths, for example, offered better protection from bandits?

The word "road" needs to be qualified here. Medieval roads, in nearly all cases, consisted of dirt tracks, likely deeply rutted and potholed. The major ones traced the foundations of stone-paved paths the Romans had engineered 1,000 years before. Most of that paving had disappeared by the 12th century. Yet, since Roman engineers took advantage of the terrain contours in any given area, the routes themselves endured; many modern highways in Europe still follow parts of the old Roman roads.

The rebirth of commercial life in Europe after the 11th century added other options for pilgrims, such as newer passages to fairs and markets, a proliferation of cattle or sheep trails and well-worn footpaths between villages. The medieval pilgrim would have followed some combination of all of these tracks to Santiago de Compostela. But in no sense did he or she follow any recognized "official" path. Pilgrims simply found their way to the Santiago cathedral as best they could.

The idea of attaching names to Camino routes didn't occur until the late 19th century and only reached its current state in the years following World War II, when the Spanish government became interested in expanding tourism. The Spanish Catholic Church played a minimal role in any of this, except to continue its ancient practice of welcoming pilgrims to its cathedral in Santiago. The Church, in fact, has never concerned itself with the particular road by which pilgrims reached Santiago. This fact is key to understanding the modern Camino de Santiago. It's not actually the Church that presides over today's vast infrastructure of routes, *albergues* and signage but rather private associations and businesses working in conjunction with local and regional governments.

Within Galicia, for example, anyone can design a new Camino route, although this is typically done through private volunteer organizations known as *amigos del Camino* ("friends of the Way"). In the case of the Spiritual Variant, the route proposal came from a group known as the La Asociación de Amigos do Camiño Portugués, which won the backing of local governments. The key approvals come at the regional government level, although the Church ultimately seals the deal by adding the route to its list of roads on which pilgrims can earn their *Compostelas*, or certificates of completion.[2]

Specifically, it's the *Dirección Xeral de Patrimonio* (General Directorate for Cultural Heritage) of the Galician regional government (*Xunta de Galicia*) that approves new pilgrim routes (known as *Caminos de Peregrinación a Santiago*). It typically does this in response to petitions from associations such as the *amigos*, mayors and town councils, as well as other institutions such as parish churches or Red Cross chapters located along the proposed new trail.

While it's considered helpful if the petitioner can provide a record of medieval pilgrims once passing along the proposed passage, such documentation is not essential. In the case of the Spiritual Variant, for example, the first historical example of a pilgrim using the route comes from the 18th century. We'll say more about that in the next chapter.

Once the Xunta de Galicia acknowledges a new trail, its various agencies take on responsibility for erecting signage and holding the petitioning municipalities accountable for providing lodging and safe walkways. For example, local governments must show proper fencing to keep cattle off the trails and indicate how an ambulance could reach an injured pilgrim, if necessary.

The Galician Ministry of Cultural Affairs and its subsidiary Office of Tourism can also require local authorities to provide multi-year commitments for safe road crossings, sufficient drainage of footpaths and plans for regular trail maintenance. There are also guidelines concerning the width of walking paths and scenic vistas.

Outside of Galicia, each Spanish region is allowed to formulate its own rules and design its own Camino signage. Coordination on a national level does not exist. Only at the very end, when all the heavy lifting has been accomplished, does the Church get involved. That's when the Cathedral Chapter (college of canons) in Santiago de Compostela, which serves as an advisory board to the bishop of Santiago, instructs the Pilgrim's Office, a subsidiary of the Chapter, to include the new route among those that qualify for *Compostelas*.[3]

Why is that important? A *Compostela* is simply a document issued by the Pilgrim's Office stating that the pilgrim has walked at least the last 100 km (or ridden 200 km, for bicyclists) on one of the approved routes to Santiago de Compostela. The *peregrino* proves that by including two *sellos* (stamps) in his credentials book for each day of that final stretch. These stamps can be obtained from churches, tourist offices, *albergues*, hotels and restaurants/cafes along the way.

Most pilgrims who reach Santiago are eager to obtain this *Compostela* because it provides "official" certification that they have indeed crossed the finish line. It's something to hang on your wall and show your friends. That's why route approval is so important to all the vendors that offer lodging and food service along the Camino; they know that once those routes are published in guidebooks, the *peregrinos* will follow. And the local governments, of course, get credit for improving their area's economy.

So, how did the Spiritual Variant get included on that list, in 2013?

---

1. See Appendix Two, "The Apostle James."
2. Technically, the Church does not care if *peregrinos* walk an approved route or create their own, as long as they can prove they walked the last 100 km. It's just easier to prove that if you stick to the approved route, since the distances between points on the way are already known.
3. The canons of the Cathedral Chapter appoint the director of the Pilgrim's Office, which coordinates some of its activities with the office of the Archbishop of Santiago. For example, the Archbishop's office can authorize visiting priests to say Masses for pilgrims within Santiago's diocesan boundaries, including the cathedral and the Pilgrim's Office's own chapel. While the Pilgrim's Office is independent of any governmental unit in Spain, it does occasionally obtain public money for large projects, such as rehabbing the former cathedral warehouse into its current offices.

# A SPIRITUAL VARIANT BY DESIGN

*T*he case for the Spiritual Variant, as designed by La Asociación de Amigos do Camiño Portugués, rested on three foundations: the route's association with the Apostles James; its use by an 18th century pilgrim named Father Martín Sarmiento; and the presence of two significant religious institutions along the way. The St. James connection gets the most prominent mention in marketing materials relating to the path, which is not surprising. The raison d'être of the Camino de Santiago revolves around the Apostle James — the "Santiago" in Camino de Santiago being the Spanish word for "St. James."

Since the early Middle Ages, Catholic tradition in Spain has held that James, one of Christ's 12 disciples, preached in Spain after the Crucifixion and then returned to Palestine, where he suffered martyrdom on the orders of King Herod. In the story, a stone boat guided by angels transported James' body back to Spain, where it ended up centuries later in a crypt at the cathedral in Santiago de Compostela. This journey from Palestine to Spain became known as the *Translatio* (Latin for "transfer," or "carry over")

The *Translatio* features in the Spiritual Variant route because the body of St. James arrived in Spain at the Roman port of Iria Flavia, now the site of the modern city of Padrón. The boat could not have reached Iria Flavia by water without entering the Bay of the Arousa River, near the modern city of Vilanova de Arousa, and then proceeding up the Ulla River to the Roman port.

That's why the Spiritual Variant includes a boat ride up the Ulla River (you can also walk alongside the bank) from Vilanova de Arousa to Pontecesures, which is just a few kilometers from Padrón. In this way, the modern *peregrino* can vicariously experience part of the *Translatio*, one of the most famous episodes in the St. James tradition.

As with the entire St. James-in-Spain narrative, the *Translatio* does not rest on any contemporary historical testimony, i.e., from the first century A.D. The Bible, which is a first-century document, tells the story of James' discipleship and ends with his martyrdom in Palestine, without mentioning Spain in any context. The Spanish connection doesn't emerge in church documents until nine hundred years later, when the perilous political situation in Spain — then dominated by the Muslims from North Africa — incentivized church officials to draw pilgrims to Santiago de Compostela to highlight the city's importance to Christianity.

Sometime in the 820s, according to this tradition, a shepherd tending his flock followed a play of lights in the sky to a Christian gravesite on Mount Libredon that had once been a Roman mausoleum. He reported his discovery to the local bishop, who attributed the remains found there to St. James. Successive chapels and churches were built on the site, around which grew the city of Santiago de Compostela.

Ever since, Catholic scholars have debated among themselves whether the body in Santiago cathedral really belongs to St. James. Pope Leo XIII ruled for the affirmative in 1884. *Deus Omnipotens* (All Powerful God), the papal bull he issued, includes a lot of cautious hedging, such as, "It is said that …" and, "Tradition holds that ..." The document never actually mentions the Apostle's bones, which disappeared in the 16th century while being hidden from English raiders led by Sir Francis Drake.[1] It wasn't until 1879 that a workman in the cathedral rediscovered them.

In his proclamation, Pope Leo XIII endorsed the veneration of the Apostle and the journey that pilgrims undertake to the tomb without claiming that it held the actual body of St. James. A recent statement by the Archdiocese of Santiago de Compostela tries to sort things out for the Faithful:

> "The most important thing here is the Goal, not the Way. Jacobean Pilgrims do not go on pilgrimage for the sake of the Way.
>
> Through the Way, they do get to the Tomb of Saint James 'the Great.' Their sacrifice and suffering while journeying to Compostela are living symbols. It consists in revealing their solidarity and compromise to the Good News of Jesus, which echoes from the Apostle's Tomb: 'The time has come. The kingdom of God is near. Repent and believe the good news! (Mark 1:15)'
>
> Thus, the Way is just a means, a road, the pilgrim walks along."

Note that the statement puts more emphasis on the journey than the destination. A pilgrim's spiritual enrichment lies in undertaking the journey, rather than worshipping at the tomb per se. Regardless, from a marketing point of view, the story of St. James is central to attracting pilgrims to Santiago de Compostela. It's a great mystery of faith that still intrigues people at some level, particularly devout Christians, as they trudge the long miles to the city. By including part of the sea-borne route of the *Translatio*, the Spiritual Variant owns a vital piece of that mystery.[2]

However, if you study the Spiritual Variant on a map, you will notice that the boat ride up the Ulla River represents only 28 km of the 74-km journey. The rest involves a walking trail that begins just north of Pontevedra and passes through the towns of Poio,

Combarro, Armenteira, Ribadumia, Pontearnelas and Vilanova de Arousa. And that's where Father Sarmiento, our 18th century pilgrim, enters the picture.

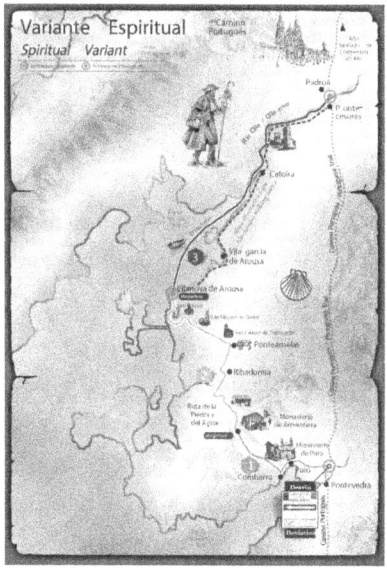

*The Spiritual Variant: Part* Translatio *and Part Father Sarmiento.*

In 1745, this Benedictine monk began walking the coastline of O Salnés, the region west of Pontevedra that includes the Arousa Bay on its westernmost side. Distinguishing features of this area include coastal inlets known as *rías,* famous for their mussel cultivation, vineyards producing Albariño wine, and some forested mountains in the interior. As he recorded in his book, *Viaje a Galicia* (Journey to Galicia), Sarmiento made his circuit of O Salnés through the towns of Poio, Sanxenxo, O Grove, Meaño, Cambados, A Illa de Arousa, Vilanova de Arousa, Vilagarcía de Arousa, Catoira, Valga and Pontecesures. From there, he continued to Santiago de Compostela and, later, explored the most northern areas of Galicia around A Coruña and Ferrol.

Father Sarmiento ventured into O Salnés to undertake a traditional pilgrimage to Santiago that included the presumed route of the *Translatio*. Having spent his childhood and youth in Pontevedra, he was also motivated by an interest in Galician language and culture. Ever since the Middle Ages, the rest of Spain has viewed Galicia as slow to modernize, the home of *meigas* (witches) and other superstitions derived from its Celtic cultural roots. The Spanish crown discouraged the use and teaching of Gallego, the region's distinctive language, a practice that continued into the 1970s.[3]

Father Sarmiento stood out in his day for wanting to preserve Gallego, and even teach it in Galician schools. He thought this would enable the local people to participate more fully in Church services, such as confession. During his travels around Galicia, he compiled notebooks of vocabulary, folk tales and songs, which is why we now have a good idea how Gallego was spoken in the 18th century.

Today, Father Sarmiento is revered in a Galicia anxious to highlight its cultural distinctiveness from the rest of Spain. When La Asociación de Amigos do Camiño Portugués built their case for the Spiritual Variant, they highlighted Father Sarmiento's 18th-century journey, even though their proposed trail did not precisely replicate his walk through O Salnés.

Where the friar ambulated around the region's coastal periphery, the modern route cuts inland from the fishing village of Combarro on the region's southeastern coast, to reach the Mosteiro de Armenteira (the monastery of Armenteira) on Mt. Castrove. Then, it continues north along the *Ruta da Pedra e da Auga* (Route of Stone and Water), a very scenic stretch of forest and abandoned water mills, before proceeding through extensive Albariño vineyards to Vilanova de Arousa. In fact, half the Spiritual Variant, from Combarro to Vilanova de Arousa, has nothing to do with either the *Translatio* or Father Sarmiento.

That brings us to the third foundation of the Spiritual Variant: reinforcing the "spiritual" aspect of the route by including two significant monasteries on its path, at Poio and Armenteira. Both of these consist of functioning religious institutions (as opposed to crumbling monuments) that feature accommodations for pilgrims and Baroque Era churches for worship. The monastery at Armenteira is particularly notable for its 18th-century cloisters and scenic mountaintop perch. The Route of Stone and Water can also be considered conducive to spiritual reflection, with its cave-like forest and burbling waterfalls.

In this way, the designers of the Spiritual Variant ended up with an appealing package: the *Translatio* of St. James, the pilgrimage of Father Sarmiento, historic monasteries and magnificent scenery.

Perhaps wishing to call more attention to Father Sarmiento, the authorities in O Salnés recently recognized a second trail, the Ruta Padre Sarmiento, that continues around the peninsula from Combarro to Vilanova de Arousa and truly replicates Sarmiento's journey.[4] This route, however, is not yet approved by the Church for receiving the *Compostela*.

---

1. For more detail on this papal bull, see https://translate.google.com/translate?hl=en&sl=es&u=https://xacopedia.com/Deus_Omnipotens&prev=search&pto=aueIt.
2. In 2019, the Pilgrims Office accepted the Xacobean Nautical Crossing as an approved section of the Camino. This sailing journey of 90 nautical miles from the port of Vigo includes the *Translatio* stretch up the Ulla River to Pontecesures. The Pilgrims Office will issue a *Compostela* for anyone who sails this journey, which represents the one exception to its 100 km walking rule.
3. Gallego and Portuguese are descendants of a common ancestor language, a branch of Proto-Romance, as is standard Spanish and Catalan. Following the end of the Spanish Civil War in 1939, dictator Francisco Franco — himself born in Ferrol, in Galicia — suppressed all regional tongues in Spain in favor of one national language.
4. The Ruta Padre Sarmiento Website can be found at: https://www.rutapadresarmiento.com. For a more detailed book of illustrations depicting Sarmeinto's journey, see https://www.osalnes.com/downloads/web-maqueta-ingle-s.pdf.

# FESTIVE PONTEVEDRA

It appears that Bina and I cannot enter the city of Pontevedra without encountering a festival.

It happened to us the previous August, during our first Camino de Santiago, when we ran into the massive celebration known as the *Feira Franca* (French Fair). The city council of Pontevedra launched this event in the early 2000s, ostensibly to commemorate the decision by King Henry IV of Castile back in the 15th century to grant the city the right to hold a tax-free market for one month each year. The festival turned out to be a wonderful occasion for people to dress up in medieval costume and party all weekend.

We did not enjoy the festivities much on our first visit because Bina came down with food poisoning and had to spend two days in bed in a downtown hotel as revelers partied in the streets below until the wee hours of the morning. A warning bell thus rang in our heads when we checked into our second-floor room at the Hotel Virgen del Camino and could hear music faintly through the windows. It was a Saturday, a weekend, so this could mean trouble. I went back downstairs to talk to the front desk clerk.

"Do you have some sort of festival in Pontevedra this weekend?" I asked her.

She looked puzzled, because she couldn't hear anything from the hotel lobby. After checking a brochure listing events in the city for the month of June, she responded.

"Yes, sir, I see here. There is a two-day rock music festival called 'Surfing the Lérez,' which is being held in a stadium a few kilometers away. This is the last day and the music is supposed to stop at 11. So, you should have no trouble sleeping tonight."

She proved correct in that assessment; the music, or musical surfing, did end shortly after 11 and we slept fine. The Lérez, by the way, is the river that empties into Pontevedra harbor. Kudos to the festival organisers for a drôle piece of marketing.

Further research on the Web that evening alerted us that *Corpus Christi* (Body of Christ), the traditional Catholic celebration of the Eucharist, began the following day. And yet another Catholic festival, celebrating San Juan (St. John), was scheduled to start two days later, on the 24th. Once again, Pontevedra had lots of festivities on tap.

By the time we arrived here, Bina and I had been on the trail for nine days, since leaving Viana do Castelo in Portugal on June 14. Per our custom, we had not walked each of those nine days. During our 2018 Camino, we had adopted a strategy of taking at least one day off for every two days of walking. We found this worked well with our general level of physical conditioning. It also provided us more time to enjoy the towns we passed through and for running necessary errands.

Following that strategy, we had designated our next day in Pontevedra, the 23rd, as one of those "down" days. This would enable us to gather our energies for the next stage of our pilgrimage, the Spiritual Variant. Once you leave Pontevedra by crossing the Lérez River at the Ponte do Burgo bridge, the turnoff to the Spiritual Variant trail is only 3 km away.

Starting the Spiritual Variant from Pontevedra dovetails nicely with the story of Father Sarmiento, who spent his childhood here before moving to Madrid at age fifteen to join the Benedictine Order. He returned to Pontevedra in 1745 to begin his pilgrimage to Santiago de Compostela with the famous walk around O Salnes, leaving the city on July 19.

1745 marked a Holy Year, or Jubilee Year, declared by the Spanish Catholic Church to honor St. James, when pilgrims to the Apostle's tomb are granted "plenary indulgence," Catholic-speak for the complete forgiveness of all sins. Such years occur when July 25, the feast day of St. James, falls on a Sunday.[1] The last one came in 2010 and the next will be in 2021.[2] In non-Holy Years, pilgrims obtain only a partial cleansing of their sins.

For modern *peregrinos*, Pontevedra is worth a tarry. The city features the second-largest old quarter in Galicia, after Santiago de Compostela itself. The historic quarter abounds in churches, secular buildings and colonnaded squares dating to Pontevedra's Golden Age, between the 12th and 16th centuries, when it was the most important port in Galicia. As the harbor began silting up in the 17th century, the city gradually fell into a decline that didn't reverse until the 1980s, when it experienced rapid growth in its service and tourism industries.

One reason that tourists flock to Pontevedra today is that its old quarter is mostly pedestrianized, with access allowed to only service vehicles and residential cars. This makes it easy to stroll from one end of town to the other, browsing the shops, tapas bars or restaurants along the way. It is European sidewalk cafe life at its best. Pontevedra has won many European urban design awards for this pedestrianization program, which began in 1999.

Pilgrims should also note that Pontevedra has been a major stopping point on the Portuguese Camino since medieval times. To commemorate that important role in the pilgrimage, the Santuario de la Virgen Peregrina was built here in the 18th century. Its stylish Baroque chapel sits on a semi-circle foundation shaped like a scallop shell (a symbol used since medieval times to represent the Camino de Santiago), the only one of its kind in Spain. A statuette of the *Divina Peregrina* (Divine Pilgrim), the virgin saint who is said to guide pilgrims to Santiago, perches on the high altar inside. This angelic figure with golden curls wears the floppy hat and money purse of a traditional pilgrim, her divine status accentuated by a white gown and green robe embroidered in gold. In her right hand, she holds a golden staff, while her left arm cradles the Baby Jesus.

What better spot for the modern *peregrino* to reflect on the journey so far and offer prayers for the future? The sanctuary also functions as a great place to obtain a *sello* (stamp) in your *credenciales* book — but more about that shortly.

After having breakfast at our hotel on the morning of the 23rd, Bina and I turned our attention to that most prosaic of chores: washing clothes. One of our survival strategies on the Camino is to wash critical items of clothing (underwear, socks and shirts) in the hotel sink and hang them to dry overnight. This generally works well for quick-dry fabrics. But for thicker fabrics, such as used for pants and skirts, we need a proper clothes dryer once in a while, which means a commercial laundromat. These can be found in major towns in Portugal and Spain.

A quick search on Google Maps located a coin-operated laundry just a few blocks from the hotel. We walked over there with our bag of soiled clothes and hung around an hour until the job was done. After depositing our now-clean clothes back in the hotel room, we set off on our second errand, which was to obtain our two *sellos* for the day.

In order to qualify for a *Compostela*, the Pilgrim's Office requires you to collect two stamps per day for every day that you spend *walking* the last 100 km to Santiago. So, how does the Spiritual Variant fit into that rule, since it includes a 28-km boat ride up the Ulla River? Doesn't that violate the rule?

The answer is that you can still get in those 100 km if you start collecting your twice-daily stamps from either the port city of

Vigo, if doing the coastal Portuguese route, or Tui, if walking the central. Bina and I had been meeting this requirement since Vigo. I hope that's clear because I've seen lots of social media posts from people who worry the Spiritual Variant boat ride will disqualify them from receiving the *Compostela*. Trust me: it won't.

Typically, collecting these *sellos* is not particularly onerous. Nearly any cafe or restaurant you pass on the trail will consent to stamp your booklet. However, proper Camino etiquette suggests that you purchase a service in exchange, for example, a cup of coffee in a cafe. Bina and I generally tried hard to obtain our *sellos* from churches, which mean more to us in terms of remembering the journey and feature more interesting designs than the typical commercial establishment.

Having been in Pontevedra the year before, we knew where to look. We started with the Santuario de la Vergin Peregrina itself, which was located just a few blocks from our hotel. On most days, a man sits at a desk by the entrance stamping *sellos* for any *peregrino* who asks for one. Except today. Peering through the front door of the chapel, we could see some locals gathered for worship but no fellow pilgrims around and no man at the desk.

Then we noticed the crowds filling up the Praza de Ferraria, the big square next to the Sanctuary. Many of these folks wore traditional costumes of black and white and carried colorful banners. Ah, yes, of course! Pontevedra was back in festival mode for Corpus Christi, which meant a disruption in daily routines and working hours.

We descended the steps from the chapel into the plaza to take a closer look. The crowd was assembling for the traditional parade, in which platforms with religious figurines (known as *passos*) are carried around town to the cathedral. Along with brass bands and Catholic banners, this parade featured a distinctly Galician twist: bagpipes. The marchers playing these instruments wore longish black shorts rather than kilts, but otherwise would have felt at home in Edinburgh.

*Bagpipes, Galician style.*

We arrived just in time. With a flourish of trumpets, the platform bearers hoisted the *passos* and began their deliberate, slow parade out of the square, swaying from side to side in a rhythmic gait. Inevitably, some marchers got out of synch, rocking to the right while others leaned left. One woman in a blue shawl and traditional black dress walked past us hand in hand with a little girl who solemnly carried her tambourine like a precious relic. Other women wore their modern Sunday best, mostly in pastel colors, while many of the men had donned black suits. We were thankful at the chance to participate in this old Spanish tradition, even from the sidelines.

*Like mother, like daughter.*

Fifteen minutes later, after the parade had passed, we had to resume our hunt for *sellos*. It was now approaching 1 p.m., and we had lunch on our minds. Unfortunately, we needed to get our stamps before the approaching afternoon siesta shut everything down. The one place we knew for sure that we could obtain a *sello* was at the tourist office, which is located in the Praza da Verdura, deep in Pontevedra's old quarter. Could we get there before it closed for the afternoon? Hustling down the narrow alleyways, we reached the office just as they were shutting the doors. The two women on station kindly stamped our credentials book, leaving us each one down and one more to go.

From our experiences the previous year, I knew that one other place to obtain a *sello* was the 16th century Santa Maria la Mayor church, on the periphery of the old town. Once again, we hurried through the narrow lanes, brushing past the lunchtime tourists, relying on Google Maps to point the way. We arrived just before 2 p.m. The church was nearly empty, since Mass had finished, and the attendants were in the process of closing the doors. Fortunately, the woman at the front desk took heed of my plea and stamped our books with a knowing smile. Glory hallelujah!

That left lunch. The restaurants and bars in the old quarter were now dense with tourists and locals drawn into town by the Corpus Christi festival. Because of Bina's diabetes, we needed to find a meal with sufficient protein and vegetables, which is not often easy in Spain. Restaurant food here is generally heavy on carbohydrates, such as rice and french fries, while the only greens available come in a mixed salad. We had to walk around for 45 minutes before finally stumbling on something called the Coren Grill, which served cafeteria-style chicken, rice and mixed vegetables that we could take back to our hotel.

Such was our frenetic afternoon in festival-obsessed Pontevedra. We didn't track our kilometers that day, but we had certainly done our share of walking for a so-called "rest' day!" Still, with our *sellos* obtained and laundry done, we were ready to embark the next day on the Spiritual Variant.

---

1. James is the English translation of the Latin *Iacomus*, which comes from the Hebrew *Ya'aqov*, or Jacob.
2. In 1122, Pope Calixtus II gave Santiago de Compostela the privilege of granting a plenary indulgence to those who visited the shrine of the Apostle in the years when the Saint's day fell on a Sunday. This is recorded in the papal bull, Regis Aeterni (Eternal Reign), issued by Pope Alexander III in 1179. Such Holy, or "Jubilee," years occur in the sequence of every 6, 5, 6 and 11 years. Typically, a Holy Year will experience a tremendous surge in pilgrims walking the Camino. But the Covid-19 pandemic in 2020 makes the outlook for 2021 uncertain.

# SAUNTERING TO COMBARRO

On Monday morning, Bina and I awoke around seven to the screeching of seagulls. This served as a good reminder of the Atlantic Ocean's proximity. When you approach Pontevedra via its southern suburbs on the Portuguese Camino, the city feels like an inland town. Yet, from its northern edge, where the Lérez River empties into the Ría de Pontevedra estuary, it's only a 40-km boat ride to the Atlantic.

We didn't mind the wake-up call because we needed to deposit our two roller bags downstairs before 8:30 a.m. On both of our Caminos, Bina and I utilized a service called Tuitrans to transport the majority of our luggage from lodging to lodging. This enabled us to walk the trail carrying only light daypacks, in which we stored some rain jackets, snacks, water and my camera (Bina shot photos with her iphone). The luggage transfer service worked well, but we could not sleep in on walking days due to the necessity of meeting that 8:30 deadline. While we never knew exactly when the Tuitrans van would show up, we couldn't risk missing a pickup.

After dropping off the bags by the hotel's front desk, we had breakfast and then hoisted our packs shortly after nine. Passing by the Sanctuary of the Virgin Pilgrim — the *sello* guy was back at his desk! — we continued following the Camino trail markers through the old quarter until we reached the Lérez River. After crossing the 12th century Ponte do Burgo bridge, we walked through some suburbs before emerging into the countryside about 15 minutes later, following a trail paralleling the railroad tracks.

Three kilometers outside of Pontevedra, we reached the concrete bridge crossing over the tracks to the left that marks the official beginning of the Spiritual Variant. Continue straight, following the rails, and you keep on the main route of the Portuguese Camino to Caldas de Reis. This is the path Bina and I had taken in 2018. If you cross the bridge to the left, you begin the Spiritual Variant. To make this clear, a yellow sign just before the overpass points to the left and is labeled "Camino Portugués A Santiago VARIANTE ESPIRITUAL." The sign helpfully shows elevations and distances between major points on the trail.

*Turn left for the Spiritual Variant.*

Crossing the bridge, we entered more wooded countryside, passing by a few scattered houses and farms, soon reaching the village of Cabaleiro. The Ingrexa de San Pedro de Campaño (Church of St. Peter of Campaño) stands at the entrance to town.[1] The origins of this structure date to the Middle Ages, but the facade you see today is the typical 18th-century Baroque makeover. The heavily weathered, algae-spotted stonework looked like it had escaped any deep cleaning in those 300 years. The guidebooks say the interior features an ornate, gold-gilded altar, but a locked door prevented us from checking it out.

Just beyond the church, we came to the Hotel Rural Campaniola, whose small restaurant we visited for a mid-morning coffee and snack. Our energies restored, we left the hotel and walked past the few other houses that constitute the village of Cabaleiro to enter a forest with a mixture of eucalyptus trees and pine trees.

You can always recognize eucalyptus by the peeling red bark and all the dead red leaves littering the path, which makes for soft treading. A first-time visitor to Galicia might wonder why eucalyptus abounds in this region, since the tree is native to Australia, and other parts of southeast Asia. A 19th-century re-forestation project gets the credit, or blame. Eucalyptus flourishes quickly and provides commercially useful timber; the oil makes it resistant to rot and decay.

The scent of eucalyptus, pungent and mentholated, gives Bina a case of the sniffles when we walk through these forests. But the real negative for these trees, as the 19th century planters soon discovered, is flammability. The oil in the bark burns easily when hit by lightning. Every summer, Spain and Portugal struggle to contain wildfires raging in their eucalyptus forests.

*Eucalyptus forest makes for good walking but bad fires.*

We emerged from this forest at the hamlet of Fragmoreira, where a clearing on a hill afforded us an expansive view of the red tiled roofs of the town of Poio, nestled along the shoreline of the Pontevedra Estuary below us. We could also discern vapor or smoke from Pontevedra's port across the water. From here, the route transitioned from forest path to paved roads and sidewalks as we descended the hill to enter the urban landscape of Poio.

This town's main claim to fame is the Monasterio de San Xoán de Poio (Monastery of St. John of Poio). This is a massive complex incorporating both a church and an attached monastery, which is currently managed by the Mercedarian order of nuns. We reached the 17th century church just as locals were celebrating the feast day of San Xoán. Vendors sold food and religious souvenirs in the courtyard as a mass was held in the sanctuary.[2]

The monastery portion of the complex offers accommodation for *peregrinos* and other travelers. Author Roy Uprichard stayed there, and comfortably so, during his walk on the Spiritual Variant, describing marble staircases inside and "seemingly endless, empty corridors."³ Although Bina and I had made reservations for the evening in Combarro, we decided to check out these accommodations ourselves, just for curiosity's sake. But we found the door to the hostel locked, probably due to the ongoing festival.

The backyard of the monastery includes the largest *horreo* (granary) in Galicia. This elongated 18th century structure, resembling a prison cell for lots of very short people, is made of stone blocks covering 112 square meters and perched on 51 squat stone pillars. Most *horreos* are much smaller.

*They don't make 'em like this anymore.*

Ubiquitous across Galicia, these structures served to keep rodents out of farmers' sacks of stored corn. Although rarely used for that purpose today, locals still keep *horreos* in their yards, partly as a touch of regional pride and partly because they have no choice. The Galician government forbids homeowners from destroying or removing *horreos*, although it will provide some financial assistance if you want to renovate one.

Upon leaving the monastery, we continued into Poio, predominantly a scene of modern, suburban sprawl. Bina and I were glad the Camino route in Poio mostly followed sidewalks, keeping us off the busy roads. But we did face some confusion at one intersection that was being torn up by a construction crew. Since the detour for the Camino path wasn't well posted, and the Wise

Pilgrim app on our phones hadn't been updated to include the detour, we had to ask for help a few times to keep on the right track.

Eventually, we found our way to the shoreline of the estuary at a public beach area, where people were shooting off fireworks, likely related to the San Xoán festival. Skirting the adjacent caravan camping ground, we reached the main road leading into Combarro. The Hotel Xeito, our family-run, three-story lodging for the night, was located on the right side of this road.

It was now about 1 p.m. We had walked 13.2 km since leaving Pontevedra four hours before. For us, that counted as a satisfactory day's walk. As a general rule, we tried to avoid covering more than 15 km in our daily Camino treks, since our preference is to "saunter" rather than "hike."

Luis, the owner of the Xeito, told us we were too early to check into our room, but offered to watch our luggage if we wished to walk into town for lunch. He recommended a restaurant called the Pedramar, which offered good seafood and a table overlooking the water. Later in the afternoon, after returning to the hotel to rest up, we explored Combarro a bit more.

Combarro is an old fishing town morphed into a popular tourist spot. The old stone and cinderblock houses of the fishermen along the waterfront have been repurposed as trendy restaurants, bars, shops and cafes. You can stroll through the narrow lanes while viewing the blue expanse of the Pontevedra Estuary in the spaces between buildings, which include dozens of *horreos*. The tourist literature claims that Combarro features more *horreos* than any other town in Galicia, about 60 in all. Back in the day, fishermen found them useful for drying fish as well as grain.

*Old Combarro: More tourists than fishermen.*

The town is packed with *cruceiros*, another distinctive feature of Galician architecture. These are stone crosses placed at crossroads or near chapels, churches and cemeteries, typically featuring images of either the Virgin Mary with child or Christ crucified. The *cruceiros* in Combarro typically represent Christ's crucifixion on their front side (with an inland orientation), and the Virgin's image at their back (facing the sea). Of the 12,000 or so *cruceiros* in Galicia overall, a goodly portion can be found in the O Salnes region.

The origin of the *cruceiros* can be traced back to the *lares*, the Roman gods of the home, hearth and roadways. To protect travelers, the Romans placed altars to the *lares* at crossroads. Native Galicians of that time, who worshipped their own gods, would light candles on these altars in the belief that they were connected with the underworld, or places where *meigas* (witches) would gather. As the Christianization of the region progressed over the centuries, people tore down the altars and replaced them with *cruceiros*, a typical example of Christian usages replacing earlier pagan symbols.

All of these features make Combarro an excellent place to linger for the night, before undertaking the steep climb to the Armenteira monastery.

1. Campaño is the name of the local parish.
2. Because the church was so crowded that day, we missed the mosaics showing various stages of the Camino Francés. See https://www.caminodesantiago.me/community/threads/enormous-camino-francés-mosaic-at-poio-monastery.68583/.
3. See, Uprichard, Roy. *Stone and Water: Walking the Spiritual Variant of the Camino de Santiago.*

# ASCENDING TO ARMENTEIRA

We always knew that our major physical challenge on the Spiritual Variant was going to be the climb up to the Mosteiro de Santa María da Armenteira. From Combarro, which sits at sea level, the trail turns inland and ascends the western slopes of Mt. Castrove, topping out at 423 meters.

Bina hikes very well on level ground, typically striding along at a faster pace than me. But hills can pose difficulty because of her asthma and diabetes. We needed to make this climb to the monastery in a comfortable, unhurried fashion, in good weather conditions. Yet, as we reviewed the situation in Combarro on the evening of June 24, the Weather Channel was predicting rain for the 26th, the day we had reserved accommodations in the monastery.

What to do? We had planned to enjoy a "down" day in Combarro on the 25th, and then walk to Armenteira the following day. Bina had gone to a lot of trouble to arrange accommodations in the monastery — speaking in Spanish to a nun over the phone — and we anticipated that staying there would be the highlight of our Spiritual Variant. The other lodging options in

Armenteira did not appeal to us: an *albergue* (hostel) or a costly hotel outside of town.

Bina made another call to the monastery and tried to switch the reservation to the 25th. But she found no vacancies in any of the 13 rooms due to the ongoing festival celebrating San Xoán. It was the 26th or nothing. We decided to make the climb on the 25th, and then taxi back to the Hotel Xeito after reaching the monastery. That left the 26th for a second taxi ride to Armenteira for check in. This new plan had the advantage of avoiding the rain while enabling us to ascend Mt. Castrove on the 25th with the lightest possible weight — me carrying water, camera and a few snacks in my day pack. Bina wouldn't have to carry anything.

Was this cheating? Bina and I didn't see it that way. Yes, we knew from reading Camino blogs and forums, that some "purists" believe the walk should be done in a properly ascetic spirit, as befits real pilgrims — no luggage transfer, stay only in communal hostels, limit your reliance on modern technology, that kind of thing. We respect those views. The pilgrimage concept, after all, is what differentiates the Camino from a typical hiking trail. Yet, we also believe that everyone must walk the Camino that is appropriate for them, based on their medical and physical conditions.

We scrupulously followed the rules when it came to walking the full distance to Santiago de Compostela. On both our 2018 and 2019 Caminos, Bina and I took care to walk the required number of kilometers between each consecutive beginning and end point on the trail. On a few occasions, however, we did see the need to utilize taxis or Uber to provide some flexibility in the order or timing of these walks. And that was the situation we faced in Combarro.

The morning of the 25th dawned slightly overcast and cool, a perfect day for climbing. We left the Xeito at 9:30 a.m. and followed our Wise Pilgrim app down the road leading into the modern shopping district of Combarro. In a moment of inattention, I missed the turnoff to the trail, which began a few blocks from the hotel. Upon discovering the mistake — what happened to that red line on my app? — we had to backtrack for a few minutes before locating the narrow lane between two houses that began the uphill walk. The sign marking the trail had become partially obscured behind some bushes.

*Not always easy to find.*

As a general rule, signage on the Spiritual Variant tends to be less conspicuous than on the main Portuguese Camino, which features yellow arrows painted on roads and buildings and periodic stone obelisks with distance plaques. The Spiritual Variant is marked with red or yellow directional arrows displayed with the white scallop shell and cross of St. James. But these directional markers either don't appear at every crossroad or are small enough to be easily overlooked. Even more so than on the main trail, we found it helpful to monitor a GPS-linked trail app when walking the Spiritual Variant.

We re-learned this lesson about a half-hour into the climb, when we missed the yellow arrow at an intersection and continued in the wrong direction along a paved country road. A fellow in a T-shirt driving a beat-up white car slowed down as he passed and asked, "Armenteira?" When I said *"Si,"* he thumbed back behind himself and said, *"primera derecha"* (first right).

Glancing down at my phone — you can't monitor the damn app every second! — I could see the man was exactly right; we had indeed missed the turn. Retracing our steps, we ended up losing about half an hour due to the mistake. From that point on, we checked for yellow signs/arrows at every intersection and consulted the app if we had any question at all about the proper route.

Much of the climb followed paved roads, which made the elevations quite walkable. And since we kept a moderate pace, Bina didn't experience any difficulties with her asthma. Along the way, we passed several farmhouses and saw a few people out tending to their grape trellises and gardens. Through occasional breaks in the tree cover, which consisted of the typical mix of eucalyptus and pine, we enjoyed sweeping views of the Pontevedra estuary down below.

We didn't hear many birds about, which we attributed to a general avian dislike of eucalyptus trees.[1] We walked most of the way in a silence broken only by the metallic murmur of an occasional car passing or farm machinery in a field. Then, ascending the road to one small village, we heard bagpipes, tambourines and drumming ahead of us.

Turning a corner, we encountered nine musicians, in traditional red, black and white Galician costume, heading our way as a few locals waved them on. We had just enough time to step aside and snap a few photos as they passed by. We had no idea what celebration or ceremony they were heading for, or where, but assumed it must have something to do with the San Xoán festival. That's the kind of serendipitous magic that can make the Camino such a delight. As veteran *peregrinos* like to say: "The Camino provides."

*Serenade on the road to Armenteira.*

Near the top of the mountain, we left the pavement to follow dirt roads and paths across a rocky outcrop. A short descent through dense forest brush then brought us right up to the stone walls enclosing the monastery compound. It had taken us four hours to walk the 13 km from the Hotel Xeito in Combarro to where the monastery perches on the western slope of Mt. Castrove, at 265 meters.

*Armenteira's Baroque Church.*

Armenteira itself is a tiny place, its few scattered houses accommodating only a few hundred inhabitants, so this massive chunk of red-roofed stonework dominates the village. As you enter the main gate, you can see directly before you, beyond the parked cars of visitors, the two-story monastery quarters with a church attached on the left. The architecture of the entire complex spans the 12th to 18th centuries. A comprehensive restoration in the 1970s and '80s, which combined new stonework with cleaned-up older blocks, produced a harmonious blend of the various styles.

Knowing that we would return the following day, Bina and I decided to limit ourselves to a brief look at the church. It was now 1:30 p.m. and lunch beckoned. The church entrance makes a great initial impression, with its doorway set in a recessed semicircle topped by a massive circular window of smaller geometric glass panes radiating around its center. Such "rose windows" are a common motif in Gothic architecture and were used in European churches up to the 19th century.[2] We found the interior cool and inviting on this hot day, with the altar featuring none of that overdone golden gilt that you see in so many other Spanish Baroque Era churches. It's a fine place to just sit quietly in the pews and reflect.

Explorations over, we exited the church to visit the Bar O Comercio, which is located across the street from the monastery's main gate. A most convenient location for tourists, this establishment features both interior and exterior dining areas. Fellow pilgrims and tourists occupied most of the outside tables, but we were able to grab one when another couple left. Bina had her favorite seafood, *zamburiñas* (variegated, or small, scallops), while I opted for a heftier cheeseburger and fries.

After lunch, we called Eduardo, a taxi driver recommended by Luis, the proprietor of the Hotel Xeito. He showed up about half an hour later and drove us down the mountain to Combarro for 20 euros. The cushy ride back felt almost sinful after our four-hour walk.

After relaxing in the hotel for the rest of the afternoon and doing some laundry in the sink, Bina and I walked into Combarro for dinner. The Pedramar was closed, for unexplained reasons, so we wandered through the old quarter looking for other restaurants, finally picking one in the open plaza near the Pedramar. We had to move under cover when it started to drizzle.

The sprinkle continued as we walked back to the hotel, where we noticed a light display strung across the street. It resembled the kind of decorations you see at Christmas time except that it featured the outline of a *horreo* (granary) rather than Santa Claus and his reindeer.

You can't get away from those *horreos* in Combarro.

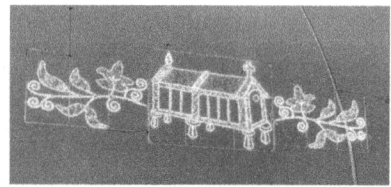

*Horreo in lights.*

---

1. See http://www.elkhornsloughctp.org/uploads/files/1108147180Suddjian-unpublished%20conference%20notes.pdf
2. For more on the "rose window" as an architectural motif, see https://en.wikipedia.org/wiki/Rose_window.

# PARADISE IN THE MONASTERY

On June 26, Wednesday, we woke up to a gray, overcast morning. It started raining after we had gone down to the Hotel Xeito's breakfast room and continued for about an hour. This would have rendered the trail up the mountain to Armenteira wet and slippery. Good call on making the walk the previous day.

Lingering for an hour or so in the breakfast room, we had time to chat with Luis, the hotel owner. Between his basic English and our elementary Spanish, we learned that he had purchased the hotel after winning a large sum in the Spanish national lottery. Lucky man! He also showed us newspaper articles with photos of him appearing in various victory celebrations with Javier Gomez Noyes, Galicia's triathlon champion, whom he described as a personal friend.[1]

Around 11, we called Eduardo, the taxi driver from the previous day, to drive us to the Armenteira monastery. It took us about half an hour to get there, compared to four hours on the previous day's walk. After Eduardo dropped us at the gate, we walked through the car park to the monastery entrance, which features an office on each side. The one on the left is operated by the tourist information service of the regional government. The other functions as a gift shop run by the monastery itself, where you can buy scented soaps and other items handcrafted by the nuns.

We went first into the tourism office to inquire about our room for the night. The two employees directed us back across the hall to the gift shop. The elderly priest behind the counter told us to take the stairs up to the second floor. A few minutes after we commenced knocking on the heavy wooden door on the landing, a middle-aged nun in black habit let us in. We were delighted to see our two roller bags sitting by the front desk. These had been transported from the Hotel Xeito that morning by Tuitrans, our luggage transfer service.

More agreeable news awaited as we followed the nun down a corridor to our room. Our frame of reference for monastery lodging at that point was the Convento de Santa Clara in Santiago de Compostela, where we had lived for two weeks in late May and early June while volunteering in the Pilgrim's Office (see Appendix One). These accommodations had turned out to be rudimentary — creaking metal frame bed in a large but musty room, with a shared bathroom in the hallway. That lodging had been provided to us free by the Pilgrim's Office, so you get what you paid for.

Our room in the Mosteiro de Santa María da Armenteira, which cost us 25 euros, could be considered luxurious by comparison: immaculately clean, firm bed, sitting area with a table and an en-suite bathroom featuring modern fixtures. It was more comfortable than many hotels we stayed in. We liked the fact that no TV was provided, which reduced the possibility of noise in the hall. In fact, complete quiet reigned during our stay. While we were aware that a few other people were staying there, we never saw or heard them. And our second floor window afforded us a calming view of the wooded courtyard and the stone walls surrounding the monastery.

Bina summed it up by saying that the place communicated benevolent peace and tranquility, making her want to stay longer. This particularly pertained to the cloisters, the colonnaded walkway in the middle of the complex, where we enjoyed walking around the open-air garden. When no other tourists intruded on the scene, the cloisters provided an ideal space for peaceful contemplation.

*Armenteira Cloisters, for a contemplative stroll.*

The nun who checked us in had made clear that only breakfast would be provided. We knew, based on our social media research, that the monastery did serve dinner at certain times of the year, such as in the peak summer months, when the nuns hosted large Christian groups. It seemed, however, that for a one-night stay, you only received breakfast.[2]

Fair enough, but where did that leave our options for lunch and dinner? Armenteira is a tiny hamlet containing only two dining establishments, the Bar O Comercio, across the street from the monastery, where we had eaten lunch the previous day, and the Fonte Cafe, one block down. From Tripadvisor reviews, we had gotten the notion that the Fonte served better food. But when we checked it out for lunch, a notice on the door announced that they were closed from June 24 to July 1.

An upscale hotel, the Pousada Armenteira, is also located on the outskirts of town. But the Pousada's Website noted that they served only breakfast. The local hostel, the Albergue de Peregrinos de Armenteira, does feature a communal kitchen, but only for staying guests.

That meant ... back to the Comercio. The cafe was a pleasant enough place, featuring both an indoor and outdoor dining area and simple food. We ended up ordering their Pilgrims Menu for both lunch and dinner. For 10 euros each, you got a plate of meat (or fish), rice and salad. Given the scarcity of eating establishments in Armenteira, our advice to fellow pilgrims is to bring some food with you so that you're not entirely dependent on what you can find in town. We congratulated ourselves on carrying enough cheese and crackers for an evening snack.

After lunch at the Commercio, we returned to the church and monastery to explore further. The church dates from the first half of the 12th century. The Baroque-style cloister and some other outbuildings were added in the 17th century, when the church itself received a makeover. The property was abandoned in 1835, after the Spanish government expropriated church holdings throughout the country. A rebuilding program, under the auspices of the Asociación de Amigos del Monasterio de Armenteira, began in 1963 and was completed in 1989, when a group of Cistercian nuns arrived from Navarre, France, to take up residence.[3] Today, the Armenteira monastery serves as both a functioning religious institution and a tourist attraction.

The dual role makes a difference. Many of the old churches in Europe that haven't been rehabilitated and are maintained mostly for historical reasons strike me as kind of depressing, with their cracked ceilings, chipped paint, and blackened stone walls. Faced with shrinking congregations and financial problems, the Catholic Church in Spain has struggled to maintain its vast collection of old buildings and religious art dating back to medieval times.[4] Armenteira monastery, after its recent restoration, retains its centuries-old look, but can now be utilized as originally intended — as a place for prayer and contemplation. You don't get distracted wondering why someone doesn't fix this wall there or clear out debris from that corner.

Bina likes to describe the Armenteira monastery as a "thin place," using Celtic terminology that denotes a physical space where the veil between this world and the eternal is so slight that you can sense the presence of God more readily. A romantic legend attached to the place suggests others have felt the same way.

As the story goes, Don Ero, Armenteira Monastery's 12th century founder and first abbot, had implored the Virgin Mary to give him a glimpse of what heaven would be like. One day, he entered the surrounding forest and sat on a stone to listen to a bird's melodic chirping. After sitting there for a while, entranced with the beauty of the birdsong, he got up and headed back to the monastery.

He did not recognize the monk who greeted him at the door, a confusion that turned out to be mutual. As other monks came on the scene to question him, the perplexed Don Ero finally realized that he had been transported 300 years into the future — that instead of listening to that bird's song for several minutes, he had spent 300 years in Paradise. The Virgin had granted his wish to see heaven.

Bina and I capped our day at the Armenteira monastery by attending the Vespers service that evening. This was held in a small chapel accessed through the cloisters. As related in the Prologue to this book, we found ourselves mesmerized by the zen-like peacefulness of the ceremony, capped by a special Pilgrims' Prayer for all the *peregrinos* in attendance. We found particularly meaningful the nun's injunction to "open your heart to silence."

That's hard to do in the modern world, with its constant media clamor, social and otherwise. But returning to our room that night, following the Vespers service, we enjoyed the most peaceful night's sleep we've ever had on a Camino.

There's something to be said for the healing powers of silence.

---

1. For a photo of Gomez, see https://www.gettyimages.com/detail/news-photo/javier-gomez-noya-of-spain-in-action-during-the-2019-news-photo/1143713651.
2. The monastery's Website states the following: "The minimum stay is 3 nights during the months of July and August and at Easter and 2 nights the rest of the year. The maximum stay is 7 days. The inn has ten rooms with two beds, two single rooms and one triple, all of them with bathroom included, with a maximum capacity of 25 people." It seems, however, that one-night stays, such as we enjoyed are common and that the best approach is simply to inquire. See https://www.caminodesantiago.me/community/threads/hospederia-in-armenteira.69061/.
3. In English usage since about the 19th century, the term "convent" almost invariably refers to a community of women, while "monastery" and "friary" are used for men. In historical usage, "monastery" and "convent" are often interchangeable.
4. See https://www.culturalheritagelaw.org/resources/Documents/The%20Protection%20of%20Abandoned%20Cultural%20Heritage%20in%20Spain.pdf.

# WATERFALL HEAVEN

The next morning, we woke up around 8:30, got dressed, and walked down the hallway to see what the nuns had prepared for breakfast. We knew we had a short Camino walk that day, so we weren't in any hurry. The breakfast room was empty but we could tell, from plates in the sink and crumbs on the table, that two other guests had been there before us. We would have enjoyed some conversation with the other folks, if only to trade experiences. Instead, we settled down to enjoy some hard-boiled eggs, bacon, toast and yogurt with coffee in a flask that had gone lukewarm.

It wasn't until we went back to our room, finished packing and were trundling our roller bags down the hallway that we saw the nun who had checked us in the previous day. She emerged from an entrance at the other end of the corridor. Through the open door we could see another passageway lined with rooms and surmised that this was the monastery (or nunnery) proper. The section that we had been staying in contained rooms only for guests, i.e., *peregrinos* and tourists. As you would expect in a cloistered environment, the majority of nuns kept away from the guests, except for special situations, such as Vespers.

We pointed to our two roller bags and said, "Tuitrans." The nun understood that we were referring to our baggage transfer service and motioned for us to leave our luggage outside the main door to the second floor. We descended the stairs and walked out of the monastery complex to enter the church for our morning prayers, thankful that our stay in Armenteira had been so enjoyable and meaningful.

It was 9:30 a.m. when we exited the monastery gates and picked up the path to the *Ruta de la Piedra y del Agua* (Way of Stone and Water), just past the O Comercio Cafe. The morning was overcast and cool, which we found ironic. A good part of Europe had been sweltering under a massive heat wave for the previous few days. We had read on the Internet about record temperatures in France and manure piles exploding in Madrid, where temperatures had exceeded 104 degrees F. [1] Not here. On this day, the temperature never rose above 60 degrees and we didn't see any direct sun until after 3 p.m.

For this reprieve from Europe's heat wave we can thank the Atlantic Ocean breezes. Galicia is called "green Spain" because cooling moisture from the Atlantic, blowing in from the west, gets trapped in the region's mountains, producing lots of drizzle. The average annual precipitation is 1,200 mm, which is wetter than nearly anywhere else in Spain and soggier than most of inland central Europe. That gives Galicia a landscape of lush pastures and forests, similar to what you might see in Ireland or England. All that shade helps tamp down the temperature in summer.

We found that lush effect considerably magnified on the Route of Stone and Water. Starting out on this path was like venturing into a cave. The dense tree canopy overhead blocked out the sun and dripped a very fine mist, keeping the leaves under our feet damp. Moss and lichen covered the trees, coating everything in a glistening green. The ferns and semi-tropical vegetation reminded Bina and me of rain forests we had visited in Costa Rica. As the trail paralleled a fast-running stream, the sound of water burbled around us while we descended from 264 meters above sea level at Armenteira to 13 meters at the bottom.

You can walk on either side of this stream. At the beginning of the path, we came to a foot bridge that crossed over to the left side of the water. Assuming this bridge designated the main route, we made the turn. We hadn't gone far before we realized that the best views of the ruined water mills — the "stone" part of the Route of Stone and Water — were to be found on the other side.

*Waterfall Heaven on the Route of Stone and Water.*

Retracing our steps, we resumed walking on the right-hand side of the stream, which featured a succession of waterfalls. Bina, who loved photographing these falls, described this section as "waterfall heaven."

**Bina:** The *Ruta de la Piedra y del Agua* is considered the highlight of the Spiritual Variant. Even though it only a short 8.2 km, it features greater opportunities for amazing photography than the rest of the trail. The key, however, is to look behind you when walking down the path. As you descend past the waterfalls, you only see the cascading water if you look back. It's a great lesson for life — to remember to look back and appreciate what has gone by instead of always looking forward! I'm sure this section would be spectacular on a sunny day, with the sun peeping through the canopy. But we appreciated the feeling of peace and tranquility that you get from walking through a lush green landscape to the sound of running water.

Most of the mills along the stream had once been used for grinding corn. Now, they lay in picturesque ruins, 32 of them according to a sign we passed. Poking around these ruins is the main diversion for people walking the trail, which includes lots of Spanish day trekkers. Typically, you will see an old grinding stone covered with green lichen in the middle of a room with a rusting crank in the corner. These stones make for a fine place to sit down and contemplate your surroundings.

*Sitting down on the job.*

Illustrated signs provide details of how the mills were constructed and the history associated with them. These info boards are mostly in Spanish, but a few included English translations. One described, with illustrations, how a sawmill on the stream operated with a system of levers, pulleys and wheels.

Diesel engines replaced the initial water-driven mechanism until the mill was finally abandoned.

*Down by the old mill stream.*

We marveled at some of the gigantic beetles and slugs we noticed on the trail. We photographed one fat slug that was half the size of Bina's trail runner. This provoked more memories of living in Costa Rica, which likes to tout its "biodiversity." Translation: lots of exotic birds, along with bugs that are much bigger than you'll ever see in the States.

After we reached the park at the bottom of the mountain, the vegetation thinned out. We passed picnic tables occupied by families relaxing at lunch while their children enjoyed the playground equipment. This park provides access to the trail for family groups and young couples who can park their cars in the lot before undertaking the walk up the mountain — passing *perigrinos* such as Bina and myself, who are descending the other way from Armenteira.

We followed the trail to a major highway junction dominated by the Os Castaños *taberna*, our planned stop for the day. This is a three-story building with a restaurant on the lower level located on the outskirts of the town of Ribadumia. We reached it around 2 p.m., having walked 8.5 km from the Armenteira Monastery.

More ambitious hikers can continue from here on to Vilanova de Arousa on the coast, which would add another 18 km. But exceeding 26 km in one day would have been way outside our comfort zone, which generally didn't exceed 15 km. We had been happy to *saunter* down the Route of Stone and Water and enjoy the scenery.

Although not located precisely halfway between Armenteira and Vilanova, Os Castaños offers *peregrinos* a good choice for lodging if they want to avoid continuing the walk to Vilanova.[2] We were now ready to check into our room, enjoy a nice lunch, and relax the rest of the day.

Before we crossed the street to the tavern, however, we noticed a one-room tourist information kiosk at the junction. Perfect, since we had some questions about taking the Vilanova de Arousa ferry to Pontecesures the next day. The young woman on duty, fluent in English, explained that two boat companies offered this ride: A Mare and Bahia-Sub. She recommended A Mare, saying they had a more modern boat. She offered to book for us, which we gladly accepted. We had read that the vessels sometimes filled up at Vilanova and were glad to have a firm booking. We arranged a 12:30 p.m. departure time.

We found a room to our liking on the third floor of the tavern and after unpacking, visited the restaurant downstairs. Enjoying a leisurely lunch, Bina and I watched the locals, happy to find the kitchen still open at this hour of the afternoon. You always have to be careful about that in Spain, where restaurants typically close for lunch around 3 and don't reopen for dinner until 9.

From our table, we noticed another *peregrino* enter, a stout, bulldog sort of fellow with close-cropped, light-colored hair wrapped in an American flag bandana. He spoke to the woman behind the bar, who escorted him upstairs. After he left, obviously to claim his room, Bina commented that she thought it a bit ostentatious for a fellow American traveler to flaunt his nationality like that.

"Americans traveling abroad typically don't do that," I agreed. "If anything, they're more inclined to downplay their nationality."

This mystery would linger for another day.

---

1. Yes, manure piles can explode. See https://www.spainenglish.com/2019/06/28/manure-pile-spark-wildfire/
2. An alternative is the Hostal Santa Baia, in Ribadumia, which is a little farther north and thus closer to Pontearnelas, which is roughly midway between Armenteira and Villanova de Arousa. See discussion in https://www.caminodesantiago.me/community/threads/is-there-lodging-in-pontearnelas.72249/#post-974218

# BRIDGE OF THE GODFATHERS

The next morning, a Thursday, we breakfasted in the Os Castaños tavern and hit the trail just after nine. Fine sunny weather greeted us, which felt good for the moment. My Weather Channel app, however, warned of temperatures reaching the 80s by the late afternoon. Having left the forested mountains around Armenteira, we knew that stretches of open plain awaited us on the way to Vilanova de Arousa.

Our initial path paralleling the Umia River provided convenient shade as we strolled past turtles sunning themselves on half-submerged tree trunks. The smell of earth and vegetation exuded from the muddy banks.

This part of the O Salnes region is known for vineyards cultivating albariño grapes, a white wine distinguished by tart, acidic fruitiness. Long rows of metal grape trellises lined the fields on both sides of the river, bunched with clusters of green, unripened fruit awaiting a fall harvest. Some of these vineyards appeared to be family-run; we saw a lone man spraying the vines as a woman tended chickens near the house. Others, with several tractors motoring around massive fields, were clearly major commercial operations.

Shortly after leaving Os Castaños, we passed a complex of brick buildings. A sign identified the property as the Pazo do Barrantes (Country House of Barrantes), Barrantes being the name of the hamlet where Os Castaños is situated. As I later researched on the Web, this 30-acre estate, owned by the Count of Creixell family since 1511, has been devoted to growing albariño grapes since the 1990s. It's two brands, Pazo Barrantes and La Comtesse, are distributed by the Marqués de Murrieta Company, which is based in Spain's Rioja region.

Roughly midway to Vilanova, we came to the Pontearnelas Bridge, in the town of the same name. This simple highway bridge spans the Umia River and features a pedestrian walkway on both sides. The locals call it the "Bridge of the Godfathers" because of its role in a fertility ritual. A woman wishing to conceive will approach the bridge in a procession of her friends and family carrying baskets of food. At the entrance to the bridge, they halt and wait for a man to approach from the opposite direction. When such a stray fellow crosses the bridge, he is asked to baptize the belly of the women with water dipped from the river in a scallop shell. (This shell is the symbol of St. James, the spiritual inspiration for the Camino de Santiago.) While the man is performing this service, the woman gazes at a cross erected near the bridge and says, "May God protect his family."

*Follow directions and you might end up with a little Alberto or Alberta.*

The ceremony ends with the woman's party sitting down to lunch nearby, after which all the crockery is thrown over the railing into the river. If the pregnancy evolves favorably, the stranger who performed the blessing will be designated as the godfather of the child. By custom, the baby's name must be Alberto, Alberta or Berta, in tribute to the saint honored by a cross adjacent to the bridge.[1]

"There must be a lot of little Albertos or Albertas running around this area," Bina commented, as she read the plaque explaining all this.

Just outside Pontearnelas, at the traffic circle where the PQ-300 highway meets the EP-7903, we encountered another intriguing landmark: a large stone sculpture of four musicians in traditional Galician costume welcoming visitors to the area. The instruments depicted are bagpipes and drums. I was immediately reminded of the similarly-attired-and-equipped musicians we had encountered three days before on the climb up to the Armenteira monastery. Galicia is a region that treasures its Celtic roots.

*And the band played on.*

From this point on, the trail became a bit more challenging. We were now walking through mostly un-shaded areas that included long stretches of asphalt road. The Spanish sun shone forth in its full, unobstructed glory. The European heat wave had caught up with us in this relatively exposed, un-forested part of Galicia. This is the point in a Camino walk when the lollygagging ends, and you start feeling a bit more incentive to reach your destination. Fortunately, it's also true that "the Camino provides," as pilgrims like to say — meaning that if the Camino presents you with a challenge, a solution will also materialize.

In the village of Mouzos, we enjoyed a welcome stop at the Capela de San Pedro. This chapel announces that it caters to *peregrinos* with a display in lights above the door outlining a medieval pilgrim, complete with cloak and floppy hat. The lights had been turned off for daylight hours, but a fellow stationed at the entrance waved us in with a hearty "Bienvenido!" and asked us to sign the guestbook. Bina and I gratefully took a seat in the cool interior to enjoy a break from the heat.

*Cooling down in the Capela de San Pedro.*

Rested, we hoisted our packs again and resumed the sweaty trudge to Vilanova de Arousa. We now began to encounter more fellow pilgrims, including a large group of young Italians, about 20 of them, of what we judged to be college age. They took turns pushing a wheelchair-bound companion, a thin, bearded fellow. We enjoyed watching their high-spirited antics, as they joked among themselves and took numerous selfies at every public monument they encountered.

A few miles from the coast, and needing to get energized for the final push into Villonova, Bina and I stopped for a coffee break in the Bar Chantada, in the village of San Roque do Monte. Soon after leaving the café, we caught glimpses of the blue Arousa estuary peeking through the tree cover as we crested a hill. We rejoiced that only an hour or so of trudging remained. There followed an easy walk down to the shoreline, where the path took us north to Vilanova. We checked into our lodging for the night at 3:30 p.m., having walked 18 km since leaving the Os Castaños tavern.

Vilanova de Arousa is an attractive holiday town, with a beach that attracts visitors during the summer months and a waterfront esplanade lined with many restaurants and cafés. Behind the cheerful facade lurks a checkered past. During the 1980s, much of the Columbian cocaine pouring into Europe arrived in fast boats that dropped off their cargoes on quiet spots along this coastline.

The government finally cracked down after local parents started complaining about their teenagers getting addicted.[2] Today, Vilanova de Arousa is better known for its mussels, which are cultivated on hundreds of rafts anchored in the bay. We would get a better look at those rafts the next morning.

Bina and I had reserved a private room for ourselves in the Albergue A Salazon, a modest but comfortable hostel. While doing our laundry downstairs in the communal washing machine (no dryer), we ran into an Irish woman, Cora, who expressed unhappiness with her shared room, which had four bunk beds. She had been paired with a man who spoke English with a German accent and wore an American flag head wrap.

Oh, *that* guy. So, he was actually German?

"I walked into the room, and there he was, sitting on the bed in his boxer shorts. He didn't say much to me, but it made me very uncomfortable trying to walk about the room with him sitting there," Cora said.

One could well imagine the awkwardness of Cora, a petite, white-haired woman, trying to bed down in the same room as this big, burly German man of curious political identity.[3] One expects less-than-ideal roommates in *albergues*, but perhaps there was another option. While walking around the Salazon, Bina and I had noticed some empty rooms. Bina, who speaks passable Spanish, volunteered to talk to the proprietor, José Francisco Navia ("Fran" for short), who had previously struck us a genial fellow.

**Bina**: We knew that Fran had left the *albergue* for a few hours to run some errands. Since we didn't know when he would be returning, we used the number posted at the front desk to call him. I spoke to him in my basic Spanish and explained the situation, adding that Cora was happy to pay for a private room, if necessary. Fran was extremely understanding and said he would be there shortly to move her to a separate room. And it all turned out wonderfully: he transferred Cora to another dorm room. And since no one else showed up that evening, Cora had the room all to herself!

Cora, I should add, was one spunky *peregrina*. A single woman from the outskirts of Dublin, well into late middle age, she had walked the entire 26 km from Armenteira to Vilanova, a journey that took us two days to accomplish. She was also a veteran of the Caminos Norte, Primitivo, Francés and Plata. In Ireland, she belonged to a hiking society and had gone with them on a trip in eastern Europe called the European Peace Walk. This woman knew her way around a hiking trail.

After hanging out our laundry on a line in the side street in front of the *albergue*, as Fran had recommended, Bina and I explored the downtown waterfront area of Vilanova de Arousa, dined in one of the restaurants on the esplanade and then settled in for a comfortable night's sleep. We looked forward to our boat ride the following day, which would provide the culmination of our journey on the Spiritual Variant.

---

1. This St. Alberto is likely to be St. Albert the Great, from the 13th century. See https://en.wikipedia.org/wiki/Albertus_Magnus.
2. Lamentably, cocaine smuggling remains a flourishing business in this area. The Galician gangs who run it are simply more discreet. See https://english.elpais.com/elpais/2019/04/10/inenglish/1554879472_974974.html.
3. Germans are not known for being wildly pro-American. See https://www.pewresearch.org/global/2019/03/04/americans-and-germans-disagree-on-the-state-of-bilateral-relations-but-largely-align-on-key-international-issues/

# THE WOLF QUEEN

With the ferryboats at Vilanova de Arousa, it seems there are schedules, and then there are schedules.

Bina and I were eating our breakfast in the common room at the Salazar when Cora walked in, sounding put out. She had arranged to take the 8 a.m. ferry to Pontecesures with the Bahia-Sub company. Walking to the pier with her gear, she found the departure had been rescheduled to 9 to accommodate a large group of young Italians with a member in a wheelchair.

Young Italians ... wheelchair ... hmm. This, of course, was the same group that Bina and I had seen on the trail the day before.

This news set us to thinking. Since the scheduling of these boats seemed to be subject to change, it might make sense to grab the earliest one possible. We were eager to reach our evening's lodging, which was located 10 km beyond Pontecesures, before sundown. The safest choice, we decided, would be Bahia-Sub's now-9 a.m. boat, even though it meant canceling our 12:30 reservation with the other company, A Mare. Said cancellation did not go down well with A Mare. They complained bitterly in a response to our WhatsApp text. Competition between these two boat companies appears to be keen.

Leaving our roller bags at the hostel, for Tuitrans to pick up later that morning, we hoisted our day bags and walked out to the pier, only a few minutes distance from the hostel. We found Cora standing in a group of about 10, mostly younger, *peregrinos*. There was no boat, no ticket office and nobody from the company around to explain the situation, although some in the crowd said the boat crew had instructed them to wait at the dock until they returned. Bina and I hung around to see what would happen, hoping we'd be able to board without reservations.

*When does it leave? Your guess is as good as mine.*

The morning was chilly, the coolest we had experienced on the Spiritual Variant, with temperatures in the low 60s and a moderate wind that intensified the chill. We were glad we were wearing our Patagonia undershirts and wind-repellant rain jackets. The double-decker ferry boat finally showed up at 9:30 and we all queued to board, including the Italian group. Fortunately, it was far from full, so Bina and I had no problem getting on without a reservation. At 9:45, the crew cast off and we chugged into the estuary to take a closer look at some of the hundreds of mussel rafts anchored in lines along the banks.

Galician mussels are famous for their quality, which is facilitated by warm water temperatures, large amounts of nutrients in the water and shelter from stormy weather. More than 95% of Spanish mussel production is concentrated in five *rias* (estuaries) on the Galician coast, including at Vigo, Pontevedra and Vilanova de Arousa, with Arousa contributing more than half of that total.

One of the crew members explained, alternating between Spanish and English, how the process begins with fishermen hanging ropes from the bottom of the rafts. These ropes attract mussel seed, or "spat" (mussels in the larval stage). After the creatures grow and concentrate on the ropes, workers transfer them to new ropes covered with a socking material whose mesh enables fuller growth under the raft. In Galicia, the mussels achieve full growth in about nine months, when the fishermen use derricks to raise the now-heavily burdened ropes for harvesting.[1]

*Industrial strength mussel farming.*

We had just begun to pull away from the rafts when the boat abruptly steered a broad U-turn back to Vilanova, as we passengers looked at each other in surprise. It took several minutes before a crew member announced we were returning to dock to pick up a couple who had missed the boat. Lots of angry expostulations ensued from the *peregrinos*, most of whom planned further walking that day, a few all the way to Santiago de Compostela. This second delay would put us behind schedule.

The young couple who clambered aboard back at the Vilanova de Arousa pier seemed genuinely embarrassed by all the fuss. The man, James Riley, explained that he and his girlfriend had shown up at the dock and mentioned their situation to a company representative. But they never expected the boat to return for them — or so he claimed. Once our irritation had subsided, and we were on our way again, I sidled up to Riley for a chat, intrigued by the fact that he had boarded carrying a guitar case. He described himself as a professional musician who had recorded several CDs, the most recent in Nashville, where he had been impressed with the skill of the studio musicians.[2] After finishing that project, he had decided to take a brief vacation by walking part of the Camino before returning to London, where he lived. Bina and I saw him a few days later playing the guitar in a café in Santiago de Compostela.

Once back in the estuary, the boat skipped the mussel barge tour — no educational lecture for Riley and his girlfriend! Instead, it veered right to proceed up the Ulla River to Pontecesures. Had we turned to the left, we would have soon reached the Atlantic Ocean.

Just past where the estuary funnels into the river, we passed under the Ulla Viaduct, a composite steel and concrete truss railroad bridge that held the title for highest in the world, at 384 feet (117 meters), when first built in 2012.[3] With its massive arc across the wooded gorge, this bridge did impress. We then immediately transitioned from this modern technological marvel back to the Middle Ages. On a small stretch of beach, just past the bridge, sat a replica of a Viking long ship, incongruously parked on the sand as 21st century vacationers launched their kayaks and paddle boats into the river nearby.

*Have Viking ship, will go raiding ...*

Here's the explanation: Behind the beach sits the small town of Catoira. In the 9th century, the king of these parts built two towers facing each other on the narrowest section of the river, just past the beach. Their purpose was to prevent Viking raiders from doing their Viking thing further up the river. The boat we saw is the one used every year in a festival on the first Sunday in August, when Viking re-enactors commemorate an assault on the now-ruined towers of Catoira by Norwegian King Olaf. This activity is said to culminate with the copious spilling of blood that smells suspiciously like red wine.[4]

Our attention next turned to the stone *cruceiros* (crosses) erected on various points along the shore. These 17 monuments, the only maritime representation of the *Via Crucis* (Way of the Cross) in the world, have been donated by churches, local governments and private companies. The placement of these *cruceiros* along the route is designed to remind modern pilgrims of the *Translatio*, the legendary passage of St. James's body from Palestine to Galicia in the first century.

> **Bina:** When we boarded the boat, I was relieved that we weren't in a little bitty boat. I had seen photos of people doing the journey in a rubber dinghy and I had been dreading that we might get stuck in one of those! This boat had seats on the first deck and a large platform to stand on the top deck, where we could view the scenery pass by. It was still overcast and somewhat chilly when we

started, so I was glad we had brought our jackets. I enjoyed hearing about the mussel farming, but wasn't happy when we had to turn around to pick up Riley and his girlfriend. When we passed the stone crosses, I wished I had done more research and understood their significance. I did do my research on the Web later that evening about both the *cruceiros* and the *Translatio*.

The basis of the *Translatio* story is contained in the 12th century *Codex Calixtinus*, also known as the *Liber sancti Jacobi* (the Book of St. James). This codex collected various sermons, miracle stories and liturgical texts related to the Apostle James. It also contains descriptions of the pilgrimage route to Santiago de Compostela, along with practical advice for making the journey, and is considered the first guidebook to the Camino de Santiago.

*Remembering the* Translatio.

The *Translatio* story begins in Palestine, in 44 A.D., when King Herod ordered James beheaded. Specificity about this date comes from Catholic tradition. The Bible says, in Acts 12: 1-2, that the Apostle James suffered martyrdom on King Herod's orders but does not identify the year. Two of his companions, Teodoro and Anastasias — whose names also appear only in medieval documents, not in the Bible — then transported his body from Jerusalem to the port of Jaffa, where they loaded it aboard a boat.

Some accounts enhance the miraculous nature of the journey by affirming that this boat was built of stone. They also related that angels helped propel the craft across the Mediterranean and through the Gibraltar straits to the Galician coast, reaching the Roman port of Iria Flavia, now identified with the modern Spanish city of Padrón.[5]

The people who designed the Spiritual Variant were able to connect the modern boat ride from Vilanova de Arousa to Pontecesures with the *Translatio* because the Ulla River passage is the only way a vessel could reach Iria Flavia. Also worthy of note: Catholic tradition in the Middle Ages identified the Iria Flavia/Padrón area as the starting point of St. James' missionary work in Spain. The Santiaguino do Monte shrine on Mt. San Gregorio, overlooking Padrón, is celebrated as the spot where he first began preaching.

After Teodoro and Anastasias tied up their boat at Iria Flavia, they appealed to the local ruler, Queen Lupa (literally, the "Wolf Queen"), for help in finding a suitable burial place for the Apostle.[6] The Wolf Queen duly provided assistance, but not in a way that proved helpful to the pair. She dispatched them to Regulus, the Roman governor of Dugium, near Finisterre, who promptly had them imprisoned. It seems that Regulus served as the high priest of a pagan cult and distrusted Christian visitors.

Teodoro and Anastasias prayed for deliverance, after which their cell door miraculously opened, enabling them to escape back to Queen Lupa. Perhaps chastened (she later converted to Christianity), the queen next directed them to a sacred mountain northeast of Iria Flavia to find an appropriate burial site for the Apostle. During this journey, the pair came across a sacred bull that led them to a Roman mausoleum on the slopes of Mount Libredón, where they finally interred the body. The Apostle lay forgotten there until the 9th century, when a shepherd followed some stars to the site. A local bishop declared the bones to be that of St. James and built a shrine atop the grave, around which later grew the city of Santiago de Compostela.

That's a lot to think about as you cruise up the river to Pontecesures, although you can also just enjoy the scenery. That town's name, by the way, means "Bridge of the Caesars" in Spanish and marks the site where a Roman road crossed the Ulla River.

By noon, after more than two hours on the water (including our abortive first departure), we approached the dock at Pontecesures, just short of the modern version of that Roman bridge. As we were queueing up to disembark, Bina asked one of the boat employees to stamp our credentials booklet. We had read that these boats provide *sellos* that show a representation of the *Translatio* boat carrying the body of St. James. We thought that would be a cool stamp to have.

"I'm sorry, but we don't have that on this boat right now," he said.

Well, why not? The young man, who was assisting other customers up the gangplank, shrugged and said the captain had forgotten to bring the stamp pad.

This may seem a small thing, but Bina and I did not embrace that excuse warmly. We needed to walk off our irritation.

Technically, at least, our journey on the Spiritual Variant had ended. At Pontecesures, we rejoined the main route of the Portuguese Camino to Santiago de Compostela. From the perspective of re-enacting the Spanish segment of the *Translatio*, however, one last step remained.

It's a two-kilometer walk from Pontecesures to Padrón. After crossing the highway bridge over the Ulla River, which is called the Ponte de Padrón, we followed the streets leading out of Pontecesures in a westerly direction to the banks of the Sar River, where a highway along the eastern bank leads directly to Padrón. The Camino trail parallels the road, giving you a brief view of river and farmland before entering Padrón's suburbs.

Bina and I knew our way around this city, having spent two days here in 2018 visiting the sites associated with the story of St. James.[7] This time, we stopped only briefly out of concern for reaching our lodging before dark. Lunch took priority, following that long morning on the boat. We stopped in a grocery store to pick up bread, cheese and fruit, and then found a shady bench in the *Paseo de Espolón*, the park-like esplanade that parallels the river in the center of town.

The city's main church, the Santiago de Padrón, sits at the Paseo's northern end. After finishing lunch, we entered to take a brief look at the *pedron* (Galician for "big stone"), which is lit up in a small space underneath the altar. According to tradition, this stone served as the bollard that Teodoro and Anastasias used to secure the boat carrying St. James' body from Palestine to Iria Flavia. It is shaped, roughly, like a bollard, although a circular depression at the top also suggests a birdbath.

Some Latin engraved on the *pedron* indicates that it had initially been dedicated to Neptune, the Roman sea god. This suggests that it may have served as a focus for religious devotion in the pre-Christian period and then got re-appropriated for religious purposes in the Middle Ages. For modern visitors who want to consider what the *Translatio* means to them, the *pedron* provides a final "touchstone" — excuse the pun — before journeying on to the Apostle's final resting place in the crypt in the Santiago de Compostela cathedral.

Well, let's visit one more touchstone. A coffee shop and tapas bar called "Don Pepe II" can be found among the storefronts crowding the small plaza outside the church. The inside functions as a Camino shrine, the walls plastered with photographs of *peregrinos* who had visited over the years. Many feature the beaming face of the proprietor, Don Pepe himself, who is happy to chat with everyone who enters his shop. Bina and I had dropped in on the tousle-haired Don Pepe during the previous year's Camino.

We repeated the visit to have a quick chat and Cappuccino before resuming our walk.

It's just one of those things you do when in Padrón.

Shouldering our packs for one last time that day, we followed the yellow Camino arrows out of Padrón's northern suburbs. Just before 3 p.m., after traversing some lightly wooded farmland, we reached our lodging for the night. This was the Casa de Meixida, a family-run inn located in the village of Tarrío, about 4 km northeast of Padrón.

On June 30, a Sunday, we left the inn at 9:15 a.m. to finish the final 22.5-km segment to the cathedral in Santiago. This actually constituted the longest stretch of our 2019 Camino, requiring five hours of steady walking. We were rewarded, in the suburban outskirts of Santiago, by one last bit of "Camino magic."

The closer you get to the city, the more crowded the trail becomes with pilgrims. We were walking amid several unrelated groups speaking various European languages when we overtook a band of six musicians decked out in traditional Galician clothing. They carried a bagpipe, flute, accordion, saxophone and two drums. The three women looked rather Amish-like in their long aproned dresses — as did the men in their dark vests and black hats.

Recognizing the opportunity for an impromptu concert, the musicians halted by a wall and struck up a lively Celtic folk tune, similar to an Irish jig. Four *peregrinas* responded to the invitation by dancing in a circle, right there in the street, still wearing their backpacks and shaking their walking sticks in time to the music. People coming together spontaneously in celebration, regardless of nationality — that's definitely the Camino spirit!

*Getting into the Camino spirit.*

We finished our pilgrimage around 2 p.m. by entering Santiago's Old Quarter and threading our way through the narrow lanes to the Praza do Obradoiro. Entering this vast plaza is usually the highlight of one's Camino. You find your spot on the pavement, among the dense knots of fellow pilgrims, and gaze awestruck at the cathedral's ornate, palatial facade looming before you. It's a time to savor the rush of emotions — gratitude, joy, the triumph of reaching your goal — before digging out your cellphone for some selfies.

*Journey's end.*

Bina and I had experienced all of that in 2018, but this time felt different. Yes, we reveled in the achievement of having arrived and we took the obligatory selfies. But we did this in a perfunctory, dutiful manner, as if going through the motions. We later admitted to ourselves that our emotions had been a lot more intense the previous year. Why was that? Picking up our second *Compostela* at the Pilgrim's Office felt like checking off a box on a to-do list: okay, done, now let's go find dinner.

It took us a while to realize that we had already experienced our spiritual highs on this Camino, before arriving in Santiago. Those moments included descending the *Ruta de la Piedra y del Agua*, passing by the *cruceiros* on the boat ride to Pontecesures and, most of all, absorbing the sense of peace we found in the Armenteira Monastery. Receiving the pilgrim's blessing during the evening Vespers service in the monastery cloisters particularly glowed in our memory. Even watching the dancing *peregrinas* earlier in the day had generated more delight. Reaching the Praza do Obradoiro came as an anticlimax following those experiences.

And that is probably the strongest argument we can make for including the Spiritual Variant in your itinerary as you walk the Portuguese Way to Santiago de Compostela. The magic is there, if you just leave yourself open to it.

---

1. For more detail, see https://thefishsite.com/articles/production-methods-for-the-mediterranean-mussel.
2. For more on Riley, see https://jamesrileymusic.com/bio.
3. See http://highestbridges.com/wiki/index.php?title=Ulla_Railway_Viaduct.
4. See https://www.timenomads.com/viking-festival-in-spain-romeria-vikinga-de-catoira/.
5. Iria Flavia was situated a kilometer or so inland from the modern port city of Padrón. Silting from the river and landfill helped build up Iria Flavia's its marshy wharf area, which grew into the riverfront urban municipality now known as Padrón.
6. Why "Wolf" Queen? George D. Greenia, Professor Emeritus of Hispanic Studies at the College of William & Mary, sent me the following commentary: "The name is perhaps a sidelong slander about her pagan state and violent tendencies. *Lupus* (wolf in Latin) becomes *lope* in later Castilian, like the last name of the famous Spanish playwright, Lope de Vega. *Lope* is also found in

the root of *Guadalupe,* where the Arabic word for a water channel (*wadi*) joins with *lope* for "Wolf River."

7. There are three of these: the *Santiago de Padrón* church, which houses the *pedron* stone; the *Santiaguino do Monte* shrine; and the St. Mary's church, built on the site of the old Roman port of Iria Flavia. If you visit all three, the local tourist office will issue you a document in Latin called the *Pedronía,* bearing the subtitle, *Hic Fuit Corpus Beati Jacobi,* or, "This was the body of St. James."

# APPENDIX ONE: VOLUNTEERING IN THE PILGRIM'S OFFICE

In early 2019, before embarking upon the Camino that is the subject of this book, Bina and I spent two weeks volunteering in the *Oficina de Acogida al Peregrino* (Pilgrim's Reception Office) in Santiago de Compostela. A department of the cathedral church of the Archdiocese of Santiago, this office is responsible for issuing the document known as the *Compostela*, which certifies you have completed the pilgrimage.

I've provided the following description of our volunteer experience in order to give readers a sense of what the Camino looks like from "the other side of the fence." Most Camino authors describe how it feels to make the long trek to Santiago to receive the certificate. But what does that process look like from behind the counter, from the perspective of those people who actually issue the *Compostelas*?

We begin with the fact that most of those people on the other side of the counter are volunteers.

It's easy for a newbie *peregrino* to think the Catholic Church pays for all the infrastructure that goes into maintaining the Camino de Santiago. When you walk into the Pilgrim's Office and see 10 to 15 people sitting behind the counter, it's logical to

## APPENDIX ONE: VOLUNTEERING IN THE PILGRIM'S OFFICE

assume they are employees. In fact, only a few are paid by the church. This dependence on volunteers also extends to all the public *albergues,* or hostels run by church-affiliated associations and municipalities. The people who volunteer their time in these organizations, typically two-week stints, often come from all over the world. The Pilgrim's Office itself is likely to be staffed by young volunteers from Santiago itself combined with a few older international folks.

Most of these *voluntarios* (volunteers) serve out of a desire to "give back" to the Camino. Our walk from Porto to Santiago in 2018 had left Bina and me eager to support the continued success of this pilgrimage. The two major opportunities for giving back are working in the Pilgrim's Office or in an *albergue.*

The worker in the *albergue,* known as a *hospitalero,* typically welcomes and registers pilgrims, sometimes cooks food for them, and often cleans bathrooms and washes/changes bed linens. We had to rule out this job because Bina's diabetes and asthma render her immune system vulnerable to infections. The *albergue* environment simply poses too much risk of her getting sick, which is why we mostly stayed in private rooms or hotels during our two Caminos.

In the Pilgrim's Office, you can interact with *peregrinos* at a safer distance. Applicants approach the counter and hand over their documents. The counter remains between you and them. We also liked the fact that the church provides free lodging for the two-week stay in Santiago de Compostela, a city whose old quarter is one of the most charming in Europe.

Bina set the wheels in motion soon after we returned to the States in October 2018. From her contacts on social media, she researched the procedure for contacting the Pilgrim's Office. In January, she sent off an email application to Montse Díaz, coordinator for the Acogida Cristiana en los Caminos de Santiago (ACC). The ACC is the organization that manages volunteers for the Pilgrim's Office and church-affiliated *albergues*. This applica-

## APPENDIX ONE: VOLUNTEERING IN THE PILGRIM'S OFFICE

tion included our brief bios, including the languages we spoke and how fluently, and preferred time for volunteering, which was for any two-week period between May 19 and July 7.

We picked that time slot so that we could begin walking our own 2019 Camino by mid-July, when the weather would likely be favorable. Also, since this was our first time volunteering in the Pilgrim's Office, we wanted to avoid the peak-season crunch, which would be mid-summer to early fall. Ms. Díaz emailed back her approval on February 5, for the period May 20 to June 3, which gave us a couple of months to plan our return to Spain.

In mid-May, we flew from Atlanta to Madrid, spent a week exploring the Spanish capital, and then took the train to Santiago. After staying in an Airbnb for a few days, we moved to the lodging provided by the Pilgrim's Office on May 20. This turned out to be the Convento de Santa Clara, a massive gray stone pile of a building on the Rúa de San Roche, just outside the old quarter and only a 15 minutes' walk to the Pilgrim's Office.[1]

These accommodations turned out to be comfortable, if somewhat Spartan. Our third-floor room featured a metal frame double bed, a small table and a few wooden chairs. We had a space heater for cool nights. On hot days, we could open the window, which afforded a view of the tiled rooftops of the Old Quarter. Two other volunteers lived on the floor with us, and two more on the level below. All six of us shared the small kitchen and dining space down the hall at the end of our floor.

The hall bathroom turned out to be our major problem. It shared a wall with our bedroom and that wall included a window. Even though the window was papered over, Bina and I heard every nocturnal flush of the toilet. But we certainly hadn't expected hotel-style comfort at this price — free. We thought we were doing pretty well, given that we were staying in a convent run by an order of nuns known as the *"Poor Clares."*

More properly styled as the "Order of Poor Ladies," the Clares live a cloistered life revolving around prayer and penance in the

## APPENDIX ONE: VOLUNTEERING IN THE PILGRIM'S OFFICE

spirit of their ascetic 13th century founder, Saint Clare.[2] There are currently about 20,000 of these nuns living in 75 countries around the world.

I ran into one of these Clares while entering the main door one afternoon after running some afternoon errands. To my great surprise, since I expected nuns to be skittish of visitors, she turned to look at me and inquired if I was a *voluntario*. When I replied with *"Si,"* she asked from where. *"Estados Unidos,"* I said. She smiled and said she had learned English in school and liked it very much. "It is a very beautiful language," she said. "But I forgot very much since then."

I assured her that her English was fine — definitely better than my Spanish. We chatted a bit more in a mixture of the two languages, mostly commiserating about how one must *"practicar todos los dias* (practice every day)" when learning a new language. I could tell that she was young, perhaps early 20s. But the nun's habit encircled her face in such a tight oval that none of her features stood out, except for nose, mouth and forehead. Had I passed her on the street, *sans* habit, I would not have recognized her.

Finishing our talk, she wished me a good evening, with God's protection. When I responded in a similar vein, she asked if I was Catholic. No, I responded, identifying myself as Protestant, specifically Lutheran. She said we were all Christian. *"Si, una iglesia* (yes, one church)," I replied, although I'm not sure if that's theologically correct, from a Catholic point of view. She simply nodded and said, yes, God looks over us all.

Otherwise, we six volunteers rarely encountered any nuns, who lived in a separate portion of the complex. The one time Bina and I attended Mass in the chapel, the nuns were hidden by a screen on an upper floor behind us; we could hear them repeating the liturgy, but could not see them.

That left Bina and me to interact mostly with our fellow international volunteers during our two weeks at the convent.

# APPENDIX ONE: VOLUNTEERING IN THE PILGRIM'S OFFICE

These included Kay, a Korean-American woman; Nusha from Slovenia; Antonio, a Spaniard; and Norwegian Alex. We communicated in English, the one common language.

All of us could be classified as middle-aged. We also had some experience walking the Camino, except for Antonio, who seems to have signed up for some generic volunteer work. Nusha and Alex had also previously worked as *hospitaleros* in *albergues*. We were all respectful of each other and got along well. It helped that we worked two different shifts, morning or afternoon. That ensured we weren't always bumping into each other in the kitchen, where only one person at a time could use the stove. However, we did manage a communal meal one afternoon between shifts, with Alex cooking up a big pot of beef chunks in tomato sauce with vegetables. Antonio supplied the wine and a convivial time was had by all.

After an initial two days of introductions, training and an orientation tour of the Pilgrim's Office, we settled into our assigned jobs on May 22. For everyone except Alex, this involved issuing *Compostelas* behind the counter. He got the job of working the line because of his fluency in most of the major European languages. As *peregrinos* arrived at our building throughout the day, the line of applicants in the courtyard could get quite long. Alex's responsibility was to ask these people to be patient and have their passport and stamp booklet ready when they reached the counter. This would help keep the line moving. [3]

Alex employed a bit of "stage business" to keep this process entertaining. If he came across a group that spoke, say, German, he would flick the lobe of his ear as if turning on a radio and announce, in a big booming voice, *"Deutsch."* Then he would annunciate the rules in near-perfect German. He could also do this in Spanish, French and English, to the awe and amusement of those standing in line.

One day, a challenge boomed out from the line: "But can you say that in Norwegian?!" This man thought he'd have a little fun

## APPENDIX ONE: VOLUNTEERING IN THE PILGRIM'S OFFICE

with Alex. How many people in the world can even say "hello" in Norwegian?

"I asked him, in English and Spanish, if that was what he really wanted, and the fellow nodded intensely," Alex recalled. "The long waiting line of pilgrims around us was paying great attention now.

"So, I said *'Momentito!'* and lifted my head towards the sky. I paused in silence for a few seconds, as if in prayer, then said, *'Gracias,'* and proceeded to deliver my spiel in my native Norwegian. I have never in my life seen such a shocked face. He jumped up and down, yelled some strong profanities — in amazement, I guess — and ran up to hug me. Everyone in the courtyard was falling over with laughter."

Alex also utilized his role as "greeter" to provide assistance to those who needed it, such as an elderly American man who had been standing in line more than two hours and seemed to be at the limit of his physical endurance. Alex ushered him to the front.

"Five minutes later, the man came out of the office, kissed me on both cheeks, crying and repeatedly thanking me. He showed me his *Compostela*, which had *'In Vicario Pro'* written on it, with his wife's name underneath. This meant he had walked the Camino for his deceased wife. He also carried a small urn with her ashes, which he planned to empty into the water at the beach in Finisterre.

"Without knowing it, I had helped the man fulfill his mission of honoring his wife."

The rest of us, meanwhile, settled into a more prosaic job that can best be likened to issuing motor vehicle licenses. Sitting at desktop computers, we would press a button on our screen that flashed instructions to the next person in line at the door to proceed to our particular numbered spot at the counter. I would ask the pilgrim for his or her *credenciales* book and identification (passport or national identity card), and hand over a form to fill in the required information. This included their name, age, place of national origin, and the town they had commenced their Camino. While they worked on that, I would scan their *credenciales* book to make sure they had collected the requisite number of *sellos*, or stamps, for them to receive their *Compostela*.

This document attests, in Latin, to the following:

> *The Chapter of this Holy Apostolic and Metropolitan Cathedral of Compostela, custodian of the seal of the Altar of St. James, to all the Faithful and pilgrims who arrive from anywhere on the Orb of the Earth with an attitude of devotion or because of a vow or promise make a pilgrimage to the Tomb of the Apostle, our Patron Saint and Protector of Spain, recognizes before all who observe this document that (**Name of pilgrim**) has devotedly visited this most sacred temple having done the last hundred kilometers on foot or horseback or the last two hundred by bicycle with Christian sentiment.*
>
> *In witness whereof, I present this document with the seal of this same Holy Church.*
>
> *Issued in Santiago de Compostela on (**Day**) of (**Month**) of our Lord (**Year**)*
>
> *The Dean of the Cathedral of Santiago.*

Note the words "Christian sentiment" above. The *Compostela* is intended to be a testimony of religious devotion, which is why we asked the applicants to identify their motives in walking the Camino as "religious, spiritual or cultural." If religious or spiritual, they were granted the *Compostela*, as displayed above, in Latin. For applicants who profess cultural or touristic motives, we provided a similar document in Spanish that leaves out the religious verbiage.

For three euros, a pilgrim can also purchase a separate document, known as the "certificate of distance," which simply attests to the total kilometers walked from wherever he or she started. This document has no religious significance, which is why the

## APPENDIX ONE: VOLUNTEERING IN THE PILGRIM'S OFFICE

Pilgrim's Office charges for it. But it does provide the *peregrino* with some "bragging rights" back home, as in, hey, look how far I walked!

Filling in these *Compostelas* is not a difficult job. It does take a few minutes to scan a pdf on the desktop searching for Latin first names to insert into the document — "James," for example, becomes "*Iacomus.*" This mystifies many applicants, so I would have to explain how a Latin document requires a Latin name — if available. This only works for people whose names derive from Romance languages, i.e., based on Latin. Having studied Latin in high school, I actually got a kick out of doing these searches.

We also had to make sure that the *credenciales* book contained two *sellos* for every day spent on the last 100 km of the walk into Santiago. Generally, the entire approval process took me only about five minutes if the pilgrim spoke English. Problems could arise, however, if the person had some "unusual issues" and could speak to me only in Spanish, French, Italian, or God help me, Korean.

A typical issue would involve someone who had finally reached Santiago after doing multiple stages over several years. This is relatively common with Europeans, who spend a few weeks a year on Camino during their vacation breaks. A French person, for example, might walk one year from Le Puy in southern France to the Spanish border, then continue on from there to Burgos the next year, and finally do Burgos to Santiago in the third. That was fine; we could issue the *Compostela* as long as they fulfilled the 100 km rule. But when this applicant hands over pages and pages of stamps and starts to gabble away in, say, Italian, I would flounder.

While I do know some basic French and Spanish, I strain when people speak rapidly. Bina has a better ear for languages and became quite adept in Spanish during our years in Costa Rica. This came in handy for her because 45% of *peregrinos* applying for *Compostelas* each year are native Spaniards. She enjoyed talking to

## APPENDIX ONE: VOLUNTEERING IN THE PILGRIM'S OFFICE

them. Myself, I preferred to be approached by native English speakers, or someone from northern Europe. If a person showed me a German or Dutch passport, I could be 90% confident that they would speak enough English to get by. French and Italians less so, and Spaniards rarely.

Koreans posed the thorniest challenge. According to the Pilgrim's Office, 8,224 South Koreans received *Compostelas* in 2019, representing 2.37% of the total, just under the U.K (2.63%) but more than Ireland (1.96%). No other Asian nationality comes close in terms of Camino participation, with Taiwan at 0.47%, Japan 0.42% and China 0.31%.[4]

Unfortunately for us volunteers, many of these Koreans displayed no facility in any western language. Some could not even read western script. They would gingerly hand over their *credenciales* book as if passing on a sacred relic and look at you imploringly. It was always helpful on such occasions to be able to call on Kay to translate. By the second week of our stint, she had written out instructions in English and Korean for us to hand out to Korean applicants. From then on, we would simply point to the English and they could read the Korean translation alongside. Nusha, well-versed in European languages, also wrote up for us a translation "cheat sheet" of necessary phrases in English, Spanish, French, Italian and German.

To be clear, multilingual talent of the type that Alex or Nusha possessed is not essential for working in the Pilgrim's Office, although some basic Spanish is helpful. It always embarrassed me to have to call on the local Spanish-speaking staff for help. I could only comfort myself with the knowledge that they would likewise turn to me when English speakers confronted them with complicated issues. I suppose it represented a fair trade in the end.

Other than language, my major stress point when working in the Pilgrim's Office related to personality. I'm a classic introvert, who doesn't much enjoy chatting with people at the best of times. Dealing with a constant stream of strangers for five hours straight left me frazzled. As soon as one applicant departed, happily waving their *Compostela*, I'd be ringing the buzzer for another one to approach. Sure, we were permitted bathroom or snack breaks, but I didn't want to be seen abusing that privilege. The end of a shift had me eagerly sprinting for the door. I never would have survived working in a call center.

In my better moments, I reminded myself that service to others does require discomfort on my part, such as straining to be friendly and sociable for extended periods. That's what I signed up for. Fortunately, some pilgrim encounters did brighten my day, for one reason or another:

*The clapper.* This skinny young Korean woman came up to my counter and watched breathlessly, bouncing up and down on her toes, as I filled in her *Compostela*. After I handed it to her, she squealed with joy and clapped her hands deliriously, like a little kid who has just been visited by Santa Claus.

*Kenneth, the exportable Irishman.* After looking at his passport, I told him right away that our software could find no Latin translation for our shared first name, which is Scottish Gaelic in origin. Latin name substitution generally works with people from countries that had been part of the ancient Roman Empire. He was okay with that, adding that he had once asked his father why he had been given a name like "Kenneth," instead of something more typically Irish, such as "Sean" or "Patrick."

"My Dad used to say, 'I gave you that name because you were *for export*.' Ireland was a poor country in those days and many young people had to go overseas for jobs. My father named me Kenneth because he always intended me to go to London to work."

Kenneth ended up instead in Rochester, New York, where he spent many years at Eastman Kodak before digital photography ruined the film business. "I'm really half American," he added.

*The wilderness therapist.* I never knew that "wilderness therapy" is a profession until I met this young American, let's call him Bill,

## APPENDIX ONE: VOLUNTEERING IN THE PILGRIM'S OFFICE

who had walked the Camino Francés from St. Jean Pied de Port, a distance of 779 km. He was so fit that he typically walked 40 km in a day, twice the distance that Bina and I could manage.

"You'd leave us in the dust," I observed admiringly.

Bill explained that he spent a lot of time hiking while on the job in Washington state, where he helped sons of wealthy families get off drugs via wilderness survival training. "You need to break them down to build them up," he explained.

"These kids grow up entitled, with no sense of doing things on their own. In the wilderness, you have to learn to do everything on your own or you don't survive."

*A white-haired Slovenian woman*, 70 years old, who said she had been walking one or two Caminos every year for the past decade. What an extraordinary achievement, I marveled. What have you learned?

She replied that a long walk lasting at least a month is better than a shorter one of just a week or so. "On a true pilgrimage, you must cross some distance and suffer a little for you to receive some meaning from the experience," she said. "You need more time with your own thoughts."

Definitely food for thought.

Bina and I also experienced our share of difficult cases. These were typically people who fell afoul of the requirement that you must walk the last 100 km to Santiago, which is the one ironclad rule that the Pilgrim's Office made us enforce. I've seen cases where the Office will excuse a missing stamp or two in the *credenciales* book, but not the walking rule.

I had to deal with this unpleasant truth early in my volunteer stint when a young woman with reddish hair approached my counter. After looking at her passport, I remarked that she was the first Bulgarian pilgrim I had dealt with. This comment set her at ease and we chatted a bit as I scanned her *credenciales* book.

I then noticed that she lacked sufficient stamps for someone who had supposedly walked the Francés all the way from St. Jean

## APPENDIX ONE: VOLUNTEERING IN THE PILGRIM'S OFFICE

Pied de Port. Under my questioning, she got flustered and admitted that she had walked from St. Jean to León but then took the bus from León to Santiago "because I had no more time. I have to catch my plane to go home."

Uh oh. I carefully explained that, by our rules, she had to walk, not ride, the last 100 km, no matter how far she had walked before León. Just to be sure, I double-checked with Luis, one of the managers in the office, who confirmed that we could not give the woman a pass on this issue.

"I'm sorry," I said, as I handed the woman her *credenciales* book. "We cannot issue you the *Compostela*."

Tears welled up in her eyes as she realized the enormity of her mistake. Spinning on her heels, she stomped off. Watching her go, I felt nearly as rotten as she did. You want people to leave your counter happily clutching their *Compostela*, not cursing you.

Bina dealt with an even worse situation. An older American man, who had been standing in line nearly two hours, came up to her station explaining that he had walked the Camino on behalf of his wife, who had died 15 months before. "This *Compostela* means a lot to me!" he affirmed.

Unfortunately, after Bina questioned him about some missing *sellos*, the man revealed that he had developed knee problems on the trail and had taken a bus into Santiago at some point during the last 100 km. Bina was heartbroken to reject his *Compostela*, but once again, the rule was clear.

Then, there was the older guy who stomped up to my counter and launched some vehement French at me, ignoring my request to *"parler plus lentement s'il vous plaît"* (speak more slowly, please). He waved in front of my nose a photocopy of a *Compostela* that he had received two days before, as if that would explain everything. I couldn't make sense of it. He already had his certificate, so why the upset?

I had to summon Luis to handle the situation. Luis was Spanish but knew his way around French. He was able to ascer-

## APPENDIX ONE: VOLUNTEERING IN THE PILGRIM'S OFFICE

tain that the guy was irate because the restaurant at the Parador, a luxury hotel across from the cathedral, had refused to give him a free breakfast. It seems there's an old custom whereby the Parador offers this perk gratis to the first ten people who receive their *Compostelas* on any particular day. This fellow seemed to think that he deserved one of these free meals, even though he had not been among the first ten. After Luis explained the rules, the guy left in a huff, still clutching his photocopy — and no doubt cursing the lot of us.

I saw a better side of human nature from an Irishman named John. He had walked the Francés from St. Jean Pied de Port and wanted to acquire a certificate of distance to show to the folks back home. When I explained that this document costs three euros, John ruefully confessed that he had left his wallet at the hotel. Believing his story, I handed him two euros, all the coins I had in my pocket. A woman standing nearby, who had been watching our interaction, contributed the last euro.

"We have a saying," I explained to him, "that 'the Camino provides.'"

"Yes, I believe that!" John said fervently, before moving on to the next counter to buy his certificate. And happy to relate, he returned a half-hour later to pay me back.

On one of the last days of our two-week stint, all of the international volunteers gathered in the small chapel in the Pilgrim's Office complex for an English mass. The service was presided over by Father Manny Domingo, a Filipino priest who had blessed Bina and me during an English mass in one of the side chapels of the Santiago cathedral the year before. To our delight, Father Manny actually remembered us. "It's very good to see you back," he said.

At the end of the service, Montse Diáz, the volunteer director, handed each of us a certificate of appreciation as Father Manny read off our names. She also gave us free tickets to see the Portico of Glory, the 12th century sculptures in the Santiago cathedral

APPENDIX ONE: VOLUNTEERING IN THE PILGRIM'S OFFICE

depicting the Apocalypse that constitute one of the highlights of medieval European religious art. This enabled us to avoid the typically long lines for viewing these masterpieces, created by a craftsman known as Master Mateo.

A 10-year restoration project has uncovered some of the original paint on the Biblical figures carved on the columns and arches of the cathedral's western entrance. The revived colors gives you a better sense of how they would have appeared 800 years ago. Actual live faces seem to emerge from the columns, now that you can see the flesh tones and ruby hue on the cheeks.

That was a nice note on which to end our *voluntario* experience. However, Bina caught a cold on Saturday, probably from one of the other volunteers staying in the convent. We were scheduled to leave Santiago by train for Viana do Castelo in Portugal on Monday and needed her rested up for that trip.

For Sunday, we booked a room at the NH Collection Santiago, a luxury hotel located in the quiet suburbs near the University of Santiago de Compostela. This proved to be a wise decision because we woke up Monday to chilly rain, the worst weather since arriving in Spain at the end of May. While Bina still nursed her cold, we taxied to the train station that afternoon with her in better shape than if we had stayed in the drafty convent.

From Santiago, we caught the 3:15 p.m. train to Vigo's Guixar station, arriving an hour and 15 minutes later. After hanging around Guixar for another two hours, we boarded a yellow Portuguese train to Viana. Our car contained only two other people, an older Columbian couple sitting across the aisle from us. They spoke English well, since they frequently visited one of their daughters in Providence, R.I.

The man, Jorge Victoria, had just finished walking the nearly 800 km of the Francés from St. Jean Pied de Port all by himself, in 31 days (with no rest days). This represented quite an achievement for someone in his early 70s. He said he had undertaken the pilgrimage to honor the memory of a second daughter, who had

## APPENDIX ONE: VOLUNTEERING IN THE PILGRIM'S OFFICE

died recently. Jorge's wife did not accompany him on the walk, but arranged to meet him in Santiago. She photographed him the morning he entered the Old Quarter, to his great surprise and delight.

*Déjà Vu experience for Jorge.*

As we were talking, Jorge mentioned that Bina somehow looked a bit familiar to him. Bina, who was thinking the same thing, asked Jorge when he had received his *Compostela*. After he cited one of our last days in the Pilgrim's Office, she asked to see the document and recognized her handwriting. Jorge caught the expression on her face.

"So, you're the one who wrote it out!" he exclaimed. "Now, I remember you. It made me so happy to receive that piece of paper, after all the walking I did. I can never thank you enough!"

Basking in Jorge's delight was the best reward Bina could have had for her two weeks as a *voluntario*.

---

1. In October 2019, accommodations for volunteers at the Pilgrim's Ofice were shifted from the Santa Clara convent to new quarters attached to the *albergue* in San Lazaro, a suburb of Santiago de Compostela. See https://www.caminodesantiago.me/community/threads/pilgrim-office-volunteer-experience-update.65071/
2. For more details on Saint Clare and her order, see https://en.wikipedia.org/wiki/Clare_of_Assisi.

## APPENDIX ONE: VOLUNTEERING IN THE PILGRIM'S OFFICE

3. The process for applying for a *Compostela* changed in August 2019. Rather than queuing up in long lines at the Pilgrim's Office, as I describe, pilgrims now take a number with a QR code and can venture off-site — grab a cup of coffee in a café, for example — while waiting for their number to be called. For full details, see https://followthecamino.com/en/blog/pilgrim-office-santiago/. Plans are also afoot to enable pilgrims to scan QR codes rather than collect stamps in their *credencials* booklet to meet the distance requirements, beginning in 2021. See https://www.caminodesantiago.me/community/threads/news-related-to-the-future-of-credencials.68592/.
4. Some best-selling travel/spiritual books and reality television shows in South Korea seem to have contributed to this phenomenon. See https://www.walkingtopresence.com/home/advice/korean-edition-of-pilgrim-stories.

# APPENDIX TWO: THE APOSTLE JAMES

During his ministry, Jesus attracted 12 principal disciples, or Apostles. "Apostle" is ancient Greek for "the one who was sent away/off on a mission." This term was attached to those men for their role in assisting Jesus during his ministry and then spreading Christianity around the Mediterranean world following the crucifixion.

The Gospels list two Jameses among the twelve. To distinguish them, later church writers labelled one as "James the Greater," and the other, "James the Lesser." The biographical details on this second James are a bit fuzzy. He may or may not have been the brother or kinsman of Jesus. In any case, James the Greater is the one linked to the Camino de Santiago.

The Bible tells us a fair amount about this James, who came from Bethsaida, near the Sea of Galilee. He was the son of Zebedee, a fisherman, and Mary Salomé. James and his brother John, who was later credited with authoring the Gospel of John, became the first followers of Jesus.

Mark 1:19-20 relates how Jesus "saw James son of Zebedee and his brother John, who were in their boat mending the nets.

## APPENDIX TWO: THE APOSTLE JAMES

Immediately he called them; and they left their father Zebedee in the boat with the hired men, and followed him."

Note the reference to "hired men." This suggests the father was a step above the common run of fishermen, since he could afford to crew his boat. Zebedee steps out of the story at this point.

Mary Salome, James' mother, followed Jesus as well and is mentioned by Mark as present at the crucifixion and the subsequent opening of Christ's empty tomb.

Jesus seems to have had a special fondness for the two brothers, particularly John. The Gospels describe him several times as "the beloved disciple." Both of them, along with Peter, were privileged to witness Jesus' Transfiguration. As the four of them climbed a mountain to pray, Jesus became outlined by bright rays of light as a voice from the sky heralded him "Son," as in, "this is my Son, the Beloved; with him I am well pleased; listen to him!" (Matthew 17:5)

Jesus nicknamed the brothers the "Sons of Thunder," suggesting that they may have had a temper. Luke 9:51-56 relates how the brothers asked Jesus to rain fire down upon a Samaritan village that declined to receive him on his way to Jerusalem. Jesus, however, "turned and rebuked them."

Mark 10:35-45 tells of another rebuke to the brothers when they asked Jesus if they would be privileged to sit with him in heaven, "one at your right hand and one at your left, in your glory." Jesus responded that such a favor "is not mine to grant" but rather is reserved for the Father. In Matthew 20:20-28, however, the offending request actually comes from Mary Salome, the mother of the two brothers.

Apparently jealous of all the attention the brothers were receiving from Jesus, the other ten disciples "began to get angry with James and John," according to Mark. This prompted Jesus to lecture them as well: "You know that among the Gentiles those whom they recognize as their rulers lord it over them … but whoever wishes to become great among you must be the slave of all."

The last mention of James in the Bible involves his martyrdom following Jesus' death. As related in Acts 12:1-2: "About that time King Herod laid violent hands upon some who belonged to the church. He had James, the brother of John, killed with the sword." Some scholars have questioned this Biblical wording because a swift form of execution, such as decapitation by the sword, was typically reserved for Roman citizens — a status that famously applied to St. Paul but not to the Apostle James. It is possible, however, that James died by the sword in a crueler, more drawn-out process.

Other Apostles became martyrs as well, according to later church tradition. The fact that James' martyrdom is the only one specifically cited in the Bible suggests that he was the first to suffer this fate.

The written record on James subsequently goes silent for more than 800 years. Then, we begin to find in church documents mentions of legends, or traditions, that move the locus of the James story from Palestine all the way to the Iberian Peninsula. These likely derived from oral stories relating to James that were passed around in the centuries following Christ's death and finally written down in the ninth century.

APPENDIX TWO: THE APOSTLE JAMES

St. James in pilgrim garb. Santa Marta de Tera Parish Church, south portal, Zamora Province of Castilla y León, Spain. Dating from circa 1125-1150, this is possibly the first statue to depict Saint James with many of the accoutrements of a pilgrim. Photo: John K. Moore, Jr.

There are two threads to this tradition. One relates that James traveled to Spain before his martyrdom to evangelize in what were then the prosperous Roman provinces of Galicia and Zaragoza. The second story involves the return of his body to Spain following his execution by King Herod. It seems that a boat guided by angels carried the Apostle's remains to the Roman port of Iria Flavia (near modern Padrón). His followers then buried him further inland on the slopes of Mount Libredón in a Roman mausoleum that was likely part of a farming estate. The body lay forgotten there for nearly 900 years.

Sometime in the 820s, a shepherd tending his flock in the area followed a play of lights in the night sky to the Roman mausoleum, now repurposed as a Christian burial site but neglected and overgrown. He reported his discovery to the local

## APPENDIX TWO: THE APOSTLE JAMES

bishop, who attributed the remains found there to St. James and his followers. A shrine and later church was built on the site, around which grew the city of Santiago de Compostela. How did the city get that name?

"Santiago" is the easy part. It's the Spanish for "James," derived originally from the Hebrew form of James, "Ya'akov." Starting with "Santo" (Saint) "Yago" (James), the Spanish evolves, over time, into "Santiago." But what about "Compostela?"

The commonly accepted assumption is that this name combines two Latin words: "campus" (field) and "stellae" (of the stars). That gives us "St. James of the field of stars," a mellifluous phrasing that dovetails nicely with the shepherd discovery story.

However, it's also possible that "Compostela" actually comes from two other Latin words: "compositum" (arranged or well-ordered) and "tellus" (field). As Roman Latin evolved into popular or Vulgar Latin during the Middle Ages, the two words put together came to designate a burial ground, or cemetery, essentially a field where things are arranged. By this interpretation, Santiago de Compostela simply means "Burial Place of St. James."

By the 12th century, the crypt in Santiago de Compostela was attracting pilgrims from all over Europe. The various routes of this pilgrimage became known as the "Way of St. James," or, in Spanish, the "Camino de Santiago."

# APPENDIX THREE: LODGING ALONG THE SPIRITUAL VARIANT

For the reader's convenience, we are providing a list of our lodging choices along the Spiritual Variant, with kilometers walked between each one. By no means are we claiming that these represent the best choices available in each locality. We are simply saying that we viewed these properties as the best compromise between value and price that we could find at the time.

Also note that the Covid pandemic of 2020-21 forced many businesses along Camino routes to close, temporarily or permanently. All the properties listed below appeared to be open in May 2021, but it's best to check ahead.

1. Pontevedra to Combarro. 13.2 km. In Pontevedra, the gateway to the Spiritual Variant, we stayed at the *Hotel Virgen del Camino*, a, modern property ideally located right on the Camino path and adjacent to the historical city center. In Combarro, our choice was *Hotel Xeito*, a small, family-run lodging located close to both the Camino and the restaurants of the fishing town's touristic area. The owner is helpful and friendly.

APPENDIX THREE: LODGING ALONG THE SPIRITUAL VARIANT

2. Combarro to Armenteira. 12 km. We counted ourselves extremely fortunate to find lodging in the *Mosteiro de Armenteira*, where we enjoyed a very comfortable, clean room in extremely quiet, peaceful surroundings for 25 euros. We obtained this one-night reservation by simply calling the monastery and speaking with the nun who answered the phone. Bina's facility with Spanish helped in that conversation since the nun spoke limited English. The contact page of the monastery's Website offers ways to make bookings via telephone or email for the 13 rooms set aside for guests, all of them with bathroom included. Note that reservations may be difficult to obtain during the peak season months of July and August, when large Christian groups book the premises for multi-day stays. Alternative lodging includes the *Albergue de Peregrinos de Armenteira* and *Pousada Armenteira*, an upscale hotel on the outskirts of town.
3. Armenteira to Ribadumia. 8.5 km. The *Os Castaños Taberna* in Ribadumia offers several rooms for lodging on two floors above the tavern. These are small but perfectly adequate for a short stay. The tavern's food is quite good. A tourist information kiosk is located right across the street where you can book a reservation on the Vilanova de Arousa ferry.
4. Ribadumia to Vilanova de Arousa. 18 km. The *Albergue A Salazon* in Vilanova offered good accommodations, both bunkbeds with shared bathrooms and single rooms with ensuite facilities. The owner is friendly and helpful. From here, it's just a few minutes' walk to the pier, the departure point for the ferry to Pontecesures.
5. Pontecesures to Tarrío. 7 km. *A Casa da Meixida* is a very simple, family-owned property that offers

APPENDIX THREE: LODGING ALONG THE SPIRITUAL VARIANT

comfortable rooms in a traditional Galician farmhouse. The 22-kilometer walk from here to the cathedral in Santiago de Compostela takes about four hours.

# ACKNOWLEDGMENTS

This book is a joint project of Kenneth and Bina Cline. The two of us walked the Spiritual Variant of the Portuguese Camino together and compiled this account together.

While I wrote the basic narrative, based on notes taken at the time, Bina supplemented the story with her own recollections. She also contributed most of the photos, many of which previously appeared in her blog of our walk, entitled *Two Clines Traveling*.[1] You can see her account under "2019 Camino de Santiago." Bina also copyedited the entire work. Without her assistance, this book would not have been possible.

Another vital source of help was the Renegades Writing Group in Dunwoody, Georgia. During the Covid pandemic in 2020, this group of literary enthusiasts met once a week via Zoom video. Brad Hayes, Ed Henderson, Michael March and Harry Stern provided invaluable feedback as I polished up the chapters for publication that summer and fall. In the proper writers critique spirit, they pushed me to work harder, and reach further.

Finally, a special callout is due George D. Greenia, Professor Emeritus of Hispanic Studies at the College of William & Mary — of which I am an alumnus (class of '76). One of the world's foremost experts on medieval pilgrimages, Greenia kindly agreed to review the historical details regarding the Camino de Santiago in chapters two and three, as well as the story of St. James in Appendix Two. Professor Greenia suggested many improvements that I gratefully incorporated into my account. I am honored by his participation in this book.

Needless to say, any remaining typos and inaccuracies of fact or interpretation are entirely my own.

---

1. See https://twoclinestraveling.wordpress.com.

# ABOUT THE AUTHOR

Kenneth Cline is a former journalist who retired in July 2016 with thirty years of experience in newspaper and magazine writing, much of that devoted to financial services, history and travel. Most recently, he was managing editor of  BAI Banking Strategies magazine. He and his wife, Bina, currently live in Tavira, Portugal.

*Sauntering the Spiritual Variant of the Camino de Santiago* is one of two books Cline has written about the "Portuguese Way" of the Camino de Santiago. The other is *Sauntering to Santiago: The Camino de Santiago for Slow Walkers* (Amazon, 2019), which covers the entire coastal route from Porto to Santiago de Compostela.

He has also written a series of books covering the two years he spent in the Middle East while on a journalism fellowship. *Mr. Kennis Goes to Yemen: A Story of West Meets East* (Amazon, 2022) describes life and culture in a village in North Yemen. *Tracking the Queen of Sheba: A Travel Memoir of Yemen* (Amazon, 2016), related his adventures accompanying an archaeological expedition to the wilds of eastern Yemen in 1984. *Village on the Nile: A Travel Memoir of Egypt* describes his experiences living in a village near Luxor the previous year.

For those with comments or questions, Cline can be reached at clin8164@bellsouth.net.

ALSO BY KENNETH CLINE

Sauntering to Santiago: The Camino de Santiago for Slow Walkers
Mr. Kennis Goes to Yemen: A Story of West Meets East
Tracking the Queen of Sheba: A Travel Memoir of Yemen
Village on the Nile: A Travel Memoir of Upper Egypt

www.ingramcontent.com/pod-product-compliance
Lightning Source LLC
Chambersburg PA
CBHW061333040426
42444CB00011B/2907